Thirty One Days in Proverbs

Reflections & Questions

H. Carl Shank

About the Author

In addition to his M.Div. and Th.M. (systematics) work, H. Carl Shank has been a youth, associate, solo, staff and lead pastor in over forty years of church ministry, pastoring beginning and established congregations in Pennsylvania, Delaware, Maryland, Virginia and New York state. His passion for leadership development has resulted in mentoring numerous pastors, teaching in a number of local Bible institutes as well as serving as an adjunct faculty member of The King's College, and training InterVarsity leaders on the East Coast. Carl has been regularly sought out for his acknowledged gifts of discernment and wisdom in dealing with church issues. He had been serving as the Executive Pastor of a church in Lancaster, PA, as well as a church health consultant through NCDAmerica. He is recently retired.

Besides numerous seminars and church related articles, his recently published Bible study contributions include *Living Life God's Way: Reflections from the Psalms, Study Guide and Leader's Guide, Romans: The Glory of God As Seen in the Righteousness of God, Jonah: A Reluctant Messenger, A Needy People, and God's Amazing Grace, Esther: For Such A Time As This, A Study of God's Providence, Church Warnings! The Seven Churches of Revelation for Today,* and *Building For God: Leadership and Life Lessons from Nehemiah* available from Lulu Press, Amazon and other booksellers. Carl is married to his wonderful wife, Nancy, and has three grown, married children. He lives in the Marietta, PA area and can be reached for consulting, seminars or leadership and mentoring development at

cshanktype@gmail.com
www.carlshankconsulting.com

Table of Contents

Valuable Works on Proverbs

Other Titles by the Author

Foreword

All Truth Is God's Truth

I write a daily devotional, mostly for myself and a group of Christian leaders from various church backgrounds and missions. I am moving through Proverbs, chapter by chapter, selecting those thoughts that God especially points out to me for me.

In my musing over Proverbs, I came to Proverbs 22 noting that there is a normal division between verses 1 – 16 and 17 – 29. "Have I not written thirty sayings for you, sayings of counsel and knowledge, teaching you to be honest and to speak the truth, so that you bring back truthful reports to those you serve?" (Proverbs 22:20, 21) The "thirty sayings" according to most commentators are closely related to the Teaching of Amenemope, an Egyptian source of wisdom.[1] This does not devalue the inspiration of the Word of God or the following thirty proverbs cited, but rather reveals God is not merely Lord of Israel but also the God of all nations in all time. God can use truth found in non-Christian contexts for his honor and glory and for the instruction of his people.

Many Christians fail to properly and thoroughly integrate God's Word with truth found in their professions or work. They look at their profession, mostly in the scientific realms, as separate and distinct from biblical revelation and its authority over their work. They value God's Word as only moral authority for proper Christian behavior, but not applicable to their science or their professional work. The Society of Christian Scholars is a worldwide group of dedicated Christians in the various professions of the world, especially academic professions.[2] They see an integrated Christianity where God's created order and truths are fused and integrated with biblical truth and revelation. They see all truth as God's truth, not separate truths for a divided life between faith and science or academia. Organizations such as CMDA (Christian Medical and Dental Association) has chapters all over the country with doctors and medical personnel seeking to wed Christianity with their medical professions.[3]

When we say "all truth is God's truth," we do not mean that there is a neutral category of "truth" out there to be discovered and then brought under the authority of Scriptural revelation. What we mean is that any and all truth, no matter where it is found or uncovered or discovered, has already been revealed by the Creator God as part of his glorious creation. New "discoveries" are merely the unpacking or unveiling to our eyes and minds what God has already given to us in his created order. This is called by presuppositional Christian apologists "analogical" truth telling, where the Creator has given all truth to be used and discovered by us, his creatures.

We have this kind of "unveiling" even in the history of redemption. The Apostle Paul says it this way — "Now to him who is able to establish you in accordance with my gospel, the message I proclaim about Jesus Christ, in keeping with the revelation of the mystery hidden for long ages past." And "No, we declare God's wisdom, a mystery that has been hidden and that God destined for our glory before time began." (Romans 16:25; 1 Corinthians 2:7)

This "mystery" is not like a spy novel mystery or an unexplained phenomenon, but rather God's progressive revelation of the gospel through the ages. Paul was the one who "discovered," or rather "uncovered," this mystery of progressive redemption by divine revelation. Even in our day, we "see only a reflection as in a mirror; then we shall see face to face. Now I know in part; then I shall know fully, even as I am fully known." (1 Cor. 13:12) What is "hidden" to us due to our sinful insights and human frailty will be made known at the Last Day, when Jesus comes again and reveals everything fully to us.

The fact that God can use Egyptian wisdom writings as part of the Scriptural record should both astound and humble us. Our work is God's work. We are to do everything to the "glory of God," 1 Corinthians 10:31 declares. This means so much more than merely doing a "good job," or making a "useful discovery" or giving a medical treatment that heals a disease. It is not merely that we are to be morally upright in doing these things, but the things themselves should reflect and point people to the "weightiness" of God in this world.[4] Until and unless we as Christian doctors and scientists and IT people and garbage collectors see and integrate God's truth into what we say and do and think and discover, we are not glorifying God. We are treating the faith as a separate and almost "hidden" part of our lives and our thoughts. That, according to Rousas Rushdoony, a conservative Presbyterian Christian writer, is "intellectual schizophrenia," not biblical integration.[5]

I am watching a rerun of the TV series JAG (Judge Advocate General Corps). One episode is about the court martial of a Gulf war commander, an outspoken Christian man, claiming that this war was a war against Satan inspired Islam.[6] He had made public comments to this effect in a sermon he gave in a Baptist church in Alexandria, VA as well as in chapel after 9/11. He was found innocent of the charges against him, but the prosecuting attorney and judge cited administrative misconduct on his part and that "religion" has no place in the military, especially by commanders to their units. And the prosecutor took his comments on Islam on and noted that JIHAD or "holy war" as practiced by Islamic extremists has no part in "regular" Islamic teaching and practice. The problem with this caricature of Islam is that the Koran does indeed contain "holy war" practices against Christians and non-Islamic combatants. This has been amply proved by a Brethren in Christ Ph.D. on the subject.[7]

The question of how biblical truth and faith can influence supposedly neutral subjects has been written on extensively, though not acknowledged by academics in the various fields. Rushdoony and his followers have provided biblically based writing on various subjects, like economics.[8] I have written a paper on biblically based mathematics, citing the underlying philosophy of number theory and arithmetical processes as foreign to the Scriptures and the revelation of God's order in the universe.[9] 1 + 1 does indeed equal 2, not because of some assumed philosophy of science approach, but because God ordered it so. We can therefore trust our mathematics, for the most part, as accurately reflecting God's universe and God's standards of counting.

Does our work or profession indicate the calling and blessing and wisdom of God upon it? Many Christians would say so, but then deny that truth in the laboratory or hospital or computer room. The result of evolutionary based science, separated from God's revelation, is to make a division of truth that has never existed. When we read the Psalms about created actions, like storms and hail and snow and vapors and so forth, this is not merely poetry and thus to be taken not literally. God in his profound wisdom and providence and involvement in this world creates and orders and determines the weather and its blessings or destructive power. Gravity works because God ordained and uses it to make things fall down and not up. He is the grand "why" of universal truth. Absenting ourselves from this revealed fact makes us agnostics rather than God-glorifying Christians.

H. Carl Shank
November 15, 2021

Notes

1.   This the generally agreed upon position by Derek Kidner in the *Tyndale Commentary Series* and by Roland Murphy in the *Word Biblical Commentary Series* on Proverbs. (Donald J. Wiseman, General Ed., *Proverbs*, Vol 17, *Tyndale Commentary Series* (Tyndale Press & InterVarsity Press, 1964). Roland E. Murphy, *Proverbs*, Vol. 22 of the *Word Biblical Commentary Series* (Thomas Nelson, 1998)).

2.   Society of Christian Scholars. The Society of Christian Scholars equips Christian academics to have a missional and redemptive influence for Christ among their students, colleagues, institutions, and academic disciplines. https://scshub.net/. This is a membership driven organization open to all Christian academics globally.

3.   CMDA. This organization helps Christian healthcare students and professionals practice with ethical standards and share their faith as a part of patient treatment. https://cmda.org/. The author is a mentor and friend of Dr. Tom Grosh, the Northeast Director of CMDA.

4.   The term for "glory" or "glorious" indicates the "weightiness" or gravity of God. In the Old Testament, "Glory" generally represents Hebrew *kābôd* (כָּבוֹד)with the root idea of "heaviness" and so of "weight" or "worthiness." It is used of men to describe their wealth, splendor or reputation (though in the last sense *kābôd* is often rendered "honor"). The glory of Israel was not her armies but Yahweh (Jer. 2:11). The word could also mean the self or soul (Gen. 49:6). The most important concept is that of the glory of Yahweh. This denotes the revelation of God's being, nature and presence to mankind. (From J. D. Douglas, ed and others, *New Bible Dictionary* (Downers Grove, IL: InterVarsity Press, 1962).

5.   Rousas John Rushdoony (April 25, 1916 – February 8, 2001) was an American Calvinist philosopher, historian, and theologian. He was ordained into the Presbyterian Church of America (PCA). He is credited as being the father of Christian Reconstructionism and an inspiration for the modern Christian homeschool movement. His followers and critics have argued that his thought exerts considerable influence on the evangelical Christian right. (https://en.wikipedia.org/wiki/Christian_ reconstructionism)

6.   JAG was a nationally rated TV series from 1995–2005, with ten seasons. This episode was from Season Nine, "Fighting Words," aired on 30 April 2004.

7.   Dr. Jay Smith. Smith believes that although Western actions in the Islamic world can instigate Muslim discontent, it is the Islamic scriptures that encourage the violence. He also rues the fact that moderate Muslims are not able to challenge the radicals using scripture because he believes the radicals have the scriptural authority. (https:// en.wikipedia.org/wiki/Jay_Smith_(Christian_apologist)

8.   Dr. Gary North. He is known for his advocacy of biblical or "radically libertarian" economics and also as a theorist of dominionism and theonomy. He supports the establishment and enforcement of Bible-based religious law, a view which has put him in conflict with other libertarians. (https://en.wikipedia.org/wiki/Gary_North_ (economist).

9.   H. Carl Shank, "Why Does 1 + 1 = 2?" in *Arguing for God: A Monograph on Logic and the Christian Faith*, Lulu Press, 2018.

Thirty One Days in Proverbs

Reflections & Questions

H. Carl Shank

Introduction

Pre-DAY 1

"Our purpose is not to 'drift and dream our way through Scripture, spiritualizing this phrase or that, hoping that a few ideas will inadvertently lodge in our minds like floating sticks snagged on a river bank.' But 'our serious concentration as we seek to apply its wisdom to the nagging and inescapable pressures with which we live.'"
(Charles Swindoll, Living the Proverbs)

How one studies the Bible profoundly impacts their life before God and others. The study of what the Bible calls "wisdom literature" can fall into a "pick-and-choose" pill a day, without any regard for the overall context or way God has put certain sayings and truths together.

Indeed, we can so exhaustively seek to understand every nugget of truth in the wisdom sayings of the Bible that we fail to see the forest because of all the trees. This particular thirty-one day devotional study of the sayings of Proverbs seeks to wind a path through the myriad snatches of wisdom to see what God may be saying to you and me in a fresh and uncluttered way.

Consequently, I have approached these thirty-one wisdom chapters, asking God for what he wants to say to me for living the life He wants for me right here and right now. I have sought to avoid the cliché approach and simply take what many others have taken from these chapters as "obvious." Rather, I start with a simple prayer — "God, show me this day in this wisdom chapter what I need to see right here and right now."

Perhaps you will see differently than I do. And that is fine. But as I have shared my God-given insights with my fellow Christians, they have agreed that what God has shown me has amply applied to them as well.

As we dive into these thirty-one chapters, some introductory comments are in order.

A General Outline of Proverbs

Preface (1:1–7)

Words of Solomon and Value of Wisdom (1:8–9:18)

Proverbs of Solomon (10:1–22:16)

Proverbs of Wise Men (22:17 –24:34)

Proverbs of Solomon collected by Hezekiah's Men (25:1–29:27)

The Wisdom of Agur (30:1–33)

The Wisdom of Lemuel (31:1–31)

How Proverbs Is Organized[1]

Much of Proverbs is given to us in couplets.

"Hear, my son, your father's instruction,

and forsake not your mother's teaching"

(Proverbs 1:8)

There are four types of couplets — contrastive, completive, corresponding and comparative. The above couplet would be *completive*. The second statement "completes" the first. Note the *and*.

A *contrasting* couplet shows two sides of the same coin. Note the *but* in the example below —

"The LORD does not let the righteous go hungry,

but he thwarts the craving of the wicked."

(Proverbs 10:3)

"The sacrifice of the wicked is an abomination to the LORD,

but the prayer of the upright is acceptable to him."

(Proverbs 15:8)

In *corresponding* couplets (called "synonymous parallelism"), the two lines express the same thought using different terms —

"Give instruction to a wise man, and he will be still wiser;

teach a righteous man, and he will increase in learning."

(Proverbs 9:9)

The second statement adds depth and can stand on its own apart from the first.

Comparative couplets invite a comparison in the two statements —

"Better is a little with the fear of the LORD

than great treasure and trouble with it.
Better is a dinner of herbs where love is
than a fattened ox and hatred with it."
(Proverbs 15:16, 17)

Notice the *"better . . . than."* Other comparative statements would be cast in *"like . . . so,"* or *"as . . . so."*

The styles of poetry in each section of the book of Proverbs display the variety in the book. In chapters one through nine, we have rather lengthy poems. In the Proverbs of Solomon (10:1–22:16) we have short, pithy statements. In Proverbs of Wise Men we have brief three or four verse stanzas. Peter Krol notes that "these differences in poetic device suggest slightly different reading strategies for each division of the book."[2]

The Theology of Proverbs

In examining the opening verses of the Preface to Proverbs, Peter Krol notes that

the book of Proverbs was written to help you (1) know what wisdom is, (2) recognize wisdom when you see it, (3) do wise things, (4) keep growing, and (5) remain anchored in God's word. The wisdom of Proverbs is neither a state of maturity nor a mere body of knowledge, but a journey in the right direction—which is away from the counsels of your own heart and toward those of your Creator.[3]

Indeed, the first nine chapters of the book build an "ideological house within which the sayings of the rest of the book make sense and land with greatest force."[4]

"Wisdom has built her house;
she has hewn her seven pillars."
(Proverbs 9:1)

While most commentators have little idea as to what the reference to the "seven pillars" are exactly, many think that Solomon is referencing the principles of the first chapters of this wisdom compilation.

What is obvious in the opening stanzas is that the "fear of the Lord" is the path to knowledge, insight and wise living. It is a directional phrase that should guide our lives, now and forever. What we want out of life is so often not what God wants for us. Rather than more stuff or more pleasures, we need more wisdom. What is this "fear of the Lord?" Rather than a frightful being scared of God, it is, as some have pointed out, the Old Testament equivalent of "justification by faith in Christ" in the New Testament. It is all about receiving righteousness from God and not by our own works.[5]

In Proverbs 1, we are introduced to the way of the "wise," the "foolish," and the "simple." The wise move toward the Lord and his word. The foolish move toward themselves, finding tragedy at the end of their self-search. The simple are those standing at the crossroads of either the way of wisdom or the way of self-destruction. Derek Kidner sagely comments, "One does not stay still: a man who is emptyheaded will end up wrongheaded."[6]

It has been said by many that the Christian life is a marathon, a journey, rather than a sprint to the finish, requiring diligent searching of what God wants and wise choices made along the way. John Bunyan's famous *Pilgrim's Progress* gives word pictures to such a journey.[7] I would highly recommend its reading to modern Christians looking for God's signposts along the road to heaven and home.

I invite you to open yourselves up to all that God would show you in these thirty-one chapters of wisdom.

Notes

1. Charles R. Swindoll, "Day 2: Proverbs 1, Wisdom and Style," *Living the Proverbs: Insight for the Daily Grind* (Worthy Books, Charles R. Swindoll, Inc., 2012), 3–8 and Peter Krol, "Proverbs: A Journey in the Right Direction," *Bible Study Magazine*, July/August 2021, 42–48.

2. Krol, "A Journey," 45.

3. Krol, "Proverbs: Part 2 of 3, A Heart Shaped by God's Wisdom," Bible Study Magazine, 46.

4. Krol, "A Journey," 45.

5. See, for instance, Dan Phillips, *God's Wisdom in Proverbs* (Kress Christian Pub., 2018).

6. Derek Kidner, "Fool: The Simple," in *Proverbs: An Introduction and Commentary*, Vol. 17 (Downers Grove, IL: InterVarsity Press, 1964) — "The Hebrew word is *petî* (פְּתָאיִם in 1:4). The verb formed from this word (like our verb 'to fool') means to deceive or seduce (as in 1:10: 'if sinners entice thee'), and the *petî*, accordingly, is the kind of person who is easily led, gullible, silly. Mentally, he is naïve ('the simple believes

everything, but the prudent looks where he is going', 14:15; cf. 22:3); morally, he is wilful and irresponsible ('the waywardness of the simple shall slay them', 1:32)."

7.   John Bunyan, *The Pilgrim's Progress: Updated Edition* (Aneko Press, 2014), originally written in 1678.

Living Vertically

DAY 1

"To know wisdom and instruction, to understand words of insight, to receive instruction in wise dealing, in righteousness, justice, and equity; to give prudence to the simple, knowledge and discretion to the youth- Let the wise hear and increase in learning, and the one who understands obtain guidance . . . The fear of the LORD is the beginning of knowledge; fools despise wisdom and instruction."

(Proverbs 1:2–5, 7 ESV)

Living vertically.[1] How do you live your life? This is the question and calling of Proverbs. Sadly, too many live their lives based on the horizontal, what they can touch, taste, see and feel, what they can prove for themselves. They then get into trouble and difficulties and end up in self-destructive tendencies and God-denying ways. How then should we live?

We need to live God-ward. We are to live as created beings, dependent on the grace and mercy and instructions of God. Too often too many only look at God as some kind of extreme escape from overwhelming odds and difficulties. We only pray because we have to. We only seek the Lord when we have no other choices. Sometimes even we who are Christians live this way. We spend our time and money and talents on things here and now and live horizontally most of the time. It is living vertically that we gain righteousness, justice and equity and find true wisdom.

We need to avoid foolish choices. Living vertically means we reject those choices that dishonor God and thwart his Word and ways. We reject people who choose wayward paths that lead to trouble and ultimately to self-destruction. It's like listening to your GPS in your car about an accident ahead and choosing an alternate and safe route. Too many continue heedless and headlong into blocked traffic and hours of delays and even maybe dangerous road conditions. Those without God in their lives are like this. They think they can weather the storms of life and plunge right into dangerous and fearful situations and somehow come out unscathed. This is living foolishly and recklessly, and the consequences will match such foolishness. Are you a wise driver? Are you a wise follower of Jesus as your GPS for life?

Lord Jesus, help me choose to live vertically in all of my life and all of my choices. Deliver me from making unwise and self-destructive choices and patterns of living. Help me choose your fear and your knowledge all the time, not just in hard and difficult times. For your honor and glory.

Self Reflection & Discussion

1. Why do we live "horizontally" and not "vertically?"
2. What is the value of living "vertically," that is, applying the Bible to every facet of daily life?
3. Define "wisdom." What is the difference between Western thought and Hebraic thought?
4. Describe the God of Proverbs.
5. Why are those without God in their lives called "simple ones" and "fools?"
6. Why should it not be surprising to us the calamities that befall those without God in their lives?

Notes

1. I am indebted to Charles R. Swindoll, *Living the Proverbs: Insight for the Daily Grind* (Worthy Books, Charles R. Swindoll, Inc., 2012) for this initial thought.

Finding Wisdom

DAY 2

"Yes, if you call out for insight and raise your voice for understanding, if you seek it like silver and search for it as for hidden treasures, then you will understand the fear of the LORD and find the knowledge of God. . . . for wisdom will come into your heart, and knowledge will be pleasant to your soul; discretion will watch over you, understanding will guard you, delivering you from the way of evil, from men of perverted speech."
(Proverbs 2:3-5, 10-12 ESV)

Finding wisdom. The way of wisdom from God is not automatic. It is not blithely given at a moment's notice. We live in an instant society and hate to wait and ponder and search for anything. Wisdom, however, cannot be bought. It has to be sought out.

Wisdom comes from diligent seeking. Searching for it like looking for hidden treasure. Treasure hunters spend loads of money and time and effort looking for hidden treasure in the sea and on land. They spend a lifetime searching for wealth and honor. We as believers need to commit ourselves to the search for wisdom and discretion in all of life. This requires loads of prayer, study of the Word of God, counsel from trusted friends and mentors and gaining a growing understanding of the faith. Gaining wisdom from God is well worth such painstaking search and discovery. I wonder at times of Christians who complain that God has not shown them the way ahead. Have they sought, really sought, for it?

Wisdom resides in the heart first. Isn't that interesting? We might think of wisdom as a mental exercise only. But real and lasting and growing wisdom resides in the center of our beings, our hearts, first and foremost. Our thinking and acting proceed from our hearts. The wisdom writer of Proverbs takes a Hebraic view of gaining wisdom, making it a holistic benefit, rather than just a mental activity. It is such a holistic view of life and its activities that keeps us from sinful choices. So, it is right to ask, What does your heart tell you?

Lord God, help me search for wisdom diligently and carefully and daily. Help me through that process to not give up and claim that it is a vain search. Rather help me to know that such a diligent search will give your wisdom in the center of my being. Thank You, dear Lord, for the grace and strength for the search!

Self Reflection & Discussion
1. How diligent in your searching of Scriptures are you? Can you give examples or instances of your "diligence?"
2. Wisdom begins in the heart. Does this surprise you? What does this mean for your journey of faith in Jesus Christ?
3. Give your own definition of "wisdom."

The Way of Wisdom

DAY 3

"My son, do not lose sight of these- keep sound wisdom and discretion, and they will be life for your soul and adornment for your neck. Then you will walk on your way securely, and your foot will not stumble. If you lie down, you will not be afraid; when you lie down, your sleep will be sweet. Do not be afraid of sudden terror or of the ruin of the wicked, when it comes, for the LORD will be your confidence and will keep your foot from being caught. Do not withhold good from those to whom it is due, when it is in your power to do it."

(Proverbs 3:21-27 ESV)

The way of wisdom. One of the banes of society and worldliness is anxiety and fretfulness. People seek relief and cures through all kinds of ungodly and dangerous means, drugs, Far Eastern religions, yoga exercises and so forth. But real peace and steadiness and stability in life evades them. How does a person live in security, peace and stability? Through the wisdom that comes from God.

Godly wisdom gives security and stability, no matter what our circumstances. Those who gain wisdom from following Christ, the true Wisdom of God, find real and satisfying peace even amid the difficulties and stresses of life. This kind of wisdom secures and steadies the soul because it answers the needs and cries of the soul, made in the image of God. It resonates with what we were created for and to be. It reaches the depths of our being and gives security even through the storms of life.

Godly wisdom looks out for others and their good — "Do not withhold good from those to whom it is due, when it is in your power to do it. Do not say to your neighbor, "Go, and come again, tomorrow I will give it"- when you have it with you. Do not plan evil against your neighbor, who dwells trustingly beside you." (Proverbs 3:27-29) What God has blessed us with, we are to watch out for and help our neighbor. We are not to withhold blessing when we can give it. We are not to plan evil against our neighbor, but rather live with trust with him or her. Because we are secure in the Lord through wisdom, we have time and pleasure to watch out for our neighbor's welfare and good. Is this the way you treat your neighbor?

Lord God, again I pray to be clothed with that wisdom from above that gives such security and relief and help even in tough times. Help me live above the evils and temptations of this world and its vain attempts at peace and security. Make my heart soft toward my neighbor and help and aid when and how I can. For your honor and glory.

Self Reflection & Discussion
1. How do you experience the peace of Christ in your life?
2. Have you found the wisdom of God a comfort as you move through trials and difficulties? How so?
3. Give some practical ways you are loving your neighbor with what God has shown and given you.

Keeping Your Heart

DAY 4

"Keep your heart with all vigilance, for from it flow the springs of life. Put away from you crooked speech, and put devious talk far from you. Let your eyes look directly forward, and your gaze be straight before you. Ponder the path of your feet; then all your ways will be sure. Do not swerve to the right or to the left; turn your foot away from evil."
(Proverbs 4:23-27 ESV)

Keeping your heart. Probably one of the most difficult and challenging things is to "keep your heart." The heart is the center of wise living and right thinking. It is the fountain from which all good and unfortunately all evil spring. If the heart is right with God and others, the mind and actions and desires will be pure and helpful. How do we keep our hearts?

Keeping the heart is an intentional action. While we say we cannot know the heart, we can certainly know the effects of the heart. What we feed the heart translates into actions and desires, assumptions and attitudes. This is why old time writers like John Bunyan talked about guarding the "eye gate" and the "ear gate." What we see and hear and with whom we fellowship and frequent penetrates our hearts. This is not so much psychology as it is heart health. With what do you feed your heart?

Always look ahead. Stumbling and tripping over feet means running into obstacles ahead. The picture here is to be clear minded and focused on what God wants us to see ahead in our lives. We are to avoid dangerous rabbit trails, distractions that can trip us up or lead us astray. We are to be those whose focus is on God's Word and God's ways. We are pilgrims looking ahead to when Jesus comes again. That is our hope and focus for all of life.

Lord Jesus, help me keep my heart pure and upright for You and your honor and glory. Deliver me from rabbit trails and distractions that can ruin my focus and ultimately my heart. Keep me wedded to your Word and your ways. Always and forever.

Self Reflection & Discussion

1. How healthy is your heart in God's sight? Don't be afraid to list those areas that still need improvement.
2. "Heart" in Hebrew literature refers to the center of your being. How do you keep your "center" focused on God and his ways?
3. Do you find your life consumed by distractions? What are you doing to free yourself from these "byways?"

Beware the Prostitute!

DAY 5

"For a man's ways are before the eyes of the LORD, and he ponders all his paths. The iniquities of the wicked ensnare him, and he is held fast in the cords of his sin. He dies for lack of discipline, and because of his great folly he is led astray."

(Proverbs 5:21-23 ESV)

Beware the prostitute! This chapter in Proverbs warns a young (or even older) man about giving in to the wiles and snares of a prostitute. While the warning is for men, generally it applies to all those tempted by sexual sins and loose living. Such sins are rampant in our day and age and we need to once again hear the wisdom of Solomon, though he certainly experienced some of the consequences of such sins.

Sexual sins contaminate the whole being. They "spend" the purity and sanctity of the person involved. They violate the person God made us to be and to live. They waste our lives, even if for a moment they fill a sinful pleasure. Too many people find this out as they live with multiple sexual partners and encounters. Sexual impurity is a sin that stains the soul. While it indeed can be forgiven by God through faith in Christ, the stain and scars remain.

Sexual sins display a failure of personal discipline. One of the fruits of the Spirit in Galatians 5 is "self-control." And it is one of the chief fruits of God's Spirit in us and one of the choicest blessings. If married we are to give our sexual selves only to the one person who deserves it, and to the writer of Proverbs, it is the "wife (or husband) of one's youth." Too much divorce with too much lack of constraint breeds personal and societal failure. We who are God's people should not be one of the casualties. This is why I have always advocated rather intense (some would say severe) pre-marital counseling.

Lord Jesus, keep my thoughts and attitudes and practices pure before You especially in my sexual life. Forgive me if I have sinned in this way and redeem me and sanctify me fully. For your Name's sake.

Self Reflection & Discussion

1. Why the stringent and urgent warning about prostitutes in this wisdom literature?

2. Think about prostitution on a broader scale, rather than just sexual sins. We can "prostitute" ourselves with the ways of an ungodly, secular world. Have there been "prostitution" areas in your life that you need to give attention?

3. If married, how much and how intense was pre-marital counseling?

Seven Things God Hates

DAY 6

"There are six things that the LORD hates, seven that are an abomination to him: haughty eyes, a lying tongue, and hands that shed innocent blood, .a heart that devises wicked plans, feet that make haste to run to evil, a false witness who breathes out lies, and one who sows discord among brothers."

(Proverbs 6:16-19 ESV)

Seven things God hates. This is strong language. That God actually "hates" some things. But the perfection of his nature demands rejection and righteous anger at those things that not merely dishonor him but reject and despise him. His holiness is perfect and pure, without alloy, and cannot stand sustained sin. This is why Jesus went to the Cross for us bearing our sins and taking the righteous punishment for them. What are seven things that offend and incur God's hatred?

Sins of pride — "haughty eyes." Pride in all of its forms is a serious offense against the Creator God. Pride says I do not need God or anyone else. I am the master of my life and the captain of my soul. It is this "Invictus"[1] attitude that sadly many of our kids are peppered with and even taught from youth up. That they can do and be and want anything, and that nothing (not even God) can stop them from achieving. This is a lie of the Devil and must be seen for what it really is. Pride deserves the hatred of God who made us with human limits and surrounds us with common grace that actually sustains us every day. Beware the sin of pride.

Sins of the tongue — false witness, sowing discord among brothers. The breach of one of the Ten Commandments is so serious that perjury in jury cases can put a person in jail. Lying, cheating, telling things that break confidences and injure others are all things God will not stand for. Apart from forgiveness through Christ these sins of the tongue can eternally ruin a person. They already have created wars and rumors of wars among nations.

Sins of the heart — a heart that devises wicked schemes and the feet and hands that carry them out. This is where the problem of sinful humanity actually lies. Jesus warned against "what comes out of a person" or from the heart. The commission of acts of evil are not accidents in God's sight but rather terrible results of hearts that devise sin and evil. it is the heart that must be transformed for acts to be good and upright. This is what modern psychology and psycho-therapy refuse to acknowledge or address. This is why the gospel is so urgently needed by so many.

O Lord, help me avoid and utterly forsake such things!!
Deliver me from those remaining sins that would threaten to cause harm to others and treat them as less than your image. Help me preach and teach and uphold the gospel of grace in a world that desperately needs it today.
For your honor and glory.

Self Reflection & Discussion

1. Do you struggle with sins of pride? How so?
2. Define more precisely God's "hatred" of some things.
3. What is the difference between healthy self-confidence and prideful living and thinking?

Notes

1. *Invictus* is a poem written by William Ernest Henley (1849–1903) supposedly celebrating the power and ability of humankind to conquer even overwhelming odds. It is at variance with the biblical doctrine of depravity of nature and choice and the need for the transforming grace of God in our lives.

> Out of the night that covers me,
> Black as the Pit from pole to pole,
> I thank whatever gods may be
> For my unconquerable soul.
>
> In the fell clutch of circumstance
> I have not winced nor cried aloud.
> Under the bludgeonings of chance
> My head is bloody, but unbowed.
> Beyond this place of wrath and tears

Looms but the Horror of the shade,
And yet the menace of the years
Finds, and shall find, me unafraid.

It matters not how strait the gate,
How charged with punishments the scroll,
I am the master of my fate:
I am the captain of my soul.

A Whole Life Christianity

DAY 7

"My son, keep my words and treasure up my commandments with you;
keep my commandments and live; keep my teaching as the apple of your
eye; bind them on your fingers; write them on the tablet of your heart."
(Proverbs 7:1–3 ESV)

A whole life Christianity. The problem with much of Christianity is that it lacks staying power when confronted with seductive evil. It is a shallow, easy believism that captivates people offering them an escape from God's just judgment but little more. It is a cosmetic Christianity that lures the soul into wayward places and seizes control of their emotions and actions. I take the section on the prostitute here with her captivating ways as any false religion or spirituality that is idolatry against God.

A whole life faith is a desired lifestyle, reaching to whatever I handle and think about. It is a faith that penetrates the darkness of false teaching and philosophy and sociology and lays them bare for what they really are— seductive ways from the world against God. Note that God's commands are to be the "apple of your eyes" written on your fingers in whatever you touch or do. This means that godly thinking penetrates every facet of thinking and believing. This is not a return to what some call "old school" teaching but is relevant for the here and now and into the future. Christian faith irradiates every discipline and career choice, every job and profession, everywhere and at every time. Is that your faith today?

Such living keeps us away from actual prostitutes and the prostitution of the faith by cleverly disguised philosophy and attractive worldliness. Such philosophies are attractive, looking to take in the "simple minded" and replete with pleasurable promises that end up in hopelessness and eternal despair. It is a "comfortable" wedding joining an alien philosophy to real Bible based faith and hope. But it ends up betraying and sickening those it attracts for a while. Stay away from such prostitution of the faith!

Lord Jesus, help me adopt and hone a holistic world view Christianity that infects and informs everything else that I think about and study and practice. Deliver me from shallowness in the faith that can lead to spiritual prostitution. All for your honor and glory.

Self Reflection & Discussion
1. In what areas in your faith-walk do you see the seduction of worldly prostitution?
2. Do you follow a "whole life" Christianity? What does that mean for you?

The Blessings of Wisdom

DAY 8

"I, wisdom, dwell with prudence, and I find knowledge and discretion.
The fear of the LORD is hatred of evil. Pride and arrogance and the way
of evil and perverted speech I hate. I have counsel and sound wisdom; I
have insight; I have strength."
(Proverbs 8:12–14 ESV)

The blessings of wisdom. "Anyone with common sense would know that!" How often we have heard these words, but how untrue they appear to be in a society laced with false information, indifference and plain sinful choices. "Common sense" seems quite far away from many today because of a lack of a moral compass in their lives. What seems "obvious" is far from many people. Why? Because they lack wisdom.

Wisdom gives common sense — "I give prudence, knowledge and discretion." Those blessings are found in the bosom of wisdom that comes from the fear of God. If I am hammering a nail into a board I do not stick my thumb in the way of the hammer — common sense. If I stay up very late and get up very early, I will be tired for business or ministry the next day — common sense. If I party all the time and engage in loose living, I may indeed find myself with a sexual disease — common sense. Why people do not "get" these things is due to a severe lack of common sense and prudence in their lives. They think that they can beat the odds and trick the Devil. We should be growing not diminishing in common sense.

Wisdom comes directly from God in Christ. This is poetically stated here in Proverbs 8 and plainly a noted by the Apostle Paul -- "but we preach Christ crucified, a stumbling block to Jews and folly to Gentiles, but to those who are called, both Jews and Greeks, Christ the power of God and the wisdom of God." (1 Cor 1:23, 24) What is considered foolishness to those without God in Christ is the wisdom of God in Christ. This is ultimately why people lack common sense, prudence and real knowledge. They lack Jesus. They think they can earn or gain or inherit or buy common sense and prudence but they are simply fooling themselves.

Lord Jesus, help me this day find wisdom and common sense and prudence and knowledge in You. Help me know where real and true wisdom comes from and seek to grow in that. Help me share the gospel with others today so that can get back on the path of wisdom in their lives. For your Name's sake.

Self Reflection & Discussion
1. Here wisdom is aligned with "common sense." Do you find the wisdom that comes from God helpful in living with common sense?
2. Why do people separate God's wisdom from common sense?
3. Are you growing or diminishing in common sense wisdom? How do you know?

Wisdom's House

DAY 9

"Wisdom has built her house; she has hewn her seven pillars. . . . Come, eat of my bread and drink of the wine I have mixed. Leave your simple ways, and live, and walk in the way of insight. . . . Give instruction to a wise man, and he will be still wiser; teach a righteous man, and he will increase in learning. The fear of the LORD is the beginning of wisdom, and the knowledge of the Holy One is insight. For by me your days will be multiplied, and years will be added to your life."
(Proverbs 9:1, 5, 6, 9-11 ESV)

Wisdom's house. No one really knows what the reference to the "seven pillars" means in Proverbs 9. One writer has wryly said — "The discussion of various theories is like walking through a cemetery; one should leave them all in peace." However, I do agree with the Word Biblical Commentary that these "seven pillars" are probably a summary of what was taught in Proverbs 1-8. This chapter 9 sounds like a summary or closing note to what has gone beforehand. It closes the first section of Proverbs and opens the door to the next. So, what's the summary?

The fear of God is the beginning and essence of true wisdom. This is repeated here and referenced throughout the first eight chapters of Proverbs. We should not be surprised. This is not merely religion masquerading as knowledge, but rather knowledge found in a relationship with God through Christ, the Wisdom of God. Everything and every true knowing rests on this. Apart from this we have folly and foolishness and the resultant destructive influences of depravity and departure from God's ways.

Wisdom blossoms and grows in wise people. This has also been emphasized in chapters one through eight. It is the wise who prosper in God's sight and increasingly gain more wisdom and insight and discernment. To reject such wisdom ends up in destructive tendencies and destruction itself for the soul. The picture here of the "scoffer" is like that found in Psalm 1 — "The wicked are not so, but are like chaff that the wind drives away. Therefore the wicked will not stand in the judgment, nor sinners in the congregation of the righteous," (Psalm 1:4,5) And the advice is given — "Blessed is the man who walks not in the counsel of the wicked, nor stands in the way of sinners, nor sits in the seat of scoffers." (Psalm 1:1)

Lord God, increasingly teach me the way of true wisdom and true fear of You. Forgive me my distractions and waywardness and tendencies to follow my own heart rather than yours. Keep me wedded to your wisdom forever and ever.

Self Reflection & Discussion
1. Pause here are re-read through Proverbs 1 – 9. What new insights have you found?
2. Describe in New Testament terms the "fear of the Lord."

Wise And Foolish Words

DAY 10

"The mouth of the righteous is a fountain of life, but the mouth of the wicked conceals violence. Hatred stirs up strife, but love covers all offenses. On the lips of him who has understanding, wisdom is found, but a rod is for the back of him who lacks sense. The wise lay up knowledge, but the mouth of a fool brings ruin near."

(Proverbs 10:11–14 ESV)

Wise and foolish words. While there are numerous one verse sayings to consider in this chapter of Proverbs, I want to focus on the words one speaks. They are either wise words from a righteous person or foolish words from a babbling fool. Notice the contrasts in the chapter.

Wise words heal, store up knowledge, give security and last — "The tongue of the righteous is choice silver; the heart of the wicked is of little worth. The lips of the righteous feed many, but fools die for lack of sense." (Vv 20, 21) "The mouth of the righteous brings forth wisdom, but the perverse tongue will be cut off. The lips of the righteous know what is acceptable, but the mouth of the wicked, what is perverse." (Vv 31, 32) Wisdom comes from righteous living. They know when to speak and when to shut up. They know how to speak and how to live. They help and heal.

Foolish words conceal destructive forces, babble endlessly and will not last — "Blessings are on the head of the righteous, but the mouth of the wicked conceals violence.... The wise of heart will receive commandments, but a babbling fool will come to ruin.... Whoever winks the eye causes trouble, and a babbling fool will come to ruin. The mouth of the righteous is a fountain of life, but the mouth of the wicked conceals violence." (Vv. 6, 8, 10, 11) Those who choose foolish ways utter foolish words, words that cut and hurt and cause misery, blustery babblings that do no good to anyone. Note that much of this talk is concealed for later use to hurt and cause destruction. Or it is just plain idiotic babbling that makes little sense. What are your words like?

Lord Jesus guard what I say today. Help my words heal and promote healthy and fruitful living for you. Deliver me from "babbling" and speaking like a fool. Guard my lips and let me speak choice words that heal and help and save. For your honor and glory.

Self Reflection & Discussion
1. Why are one's "words" so important to watch?
2. Have you seen or experienced instances of foolish words doing harm or evil to people?
3. Do you pay attention to your words closely enough? Why or why not?

Righteous Living

DAY 11

"The integrity of the upright guides them, but the crookedness of the treacherous destroys them. Riches do not profit in the day of wrath, but righteousness delivers from death. The righteousness of the blameless keeps his way straight, but the wicked falls by his own wickedness. The righteousness of the upright delivers them, but the treacherous are taken captive by their lust. . . . The righteous is delivered from trouble, and the wicked walks into it instead. . . . When it goes well with the righteous, the city rejoices, and when the wicked perish there are shouts of gladness. By the blessing of the upright a city is exalted, but by the mouth of the wicked it is overthrown. . . The fruit of the righteous is a tree of life, and whoever captures souls is wise."
(Proverbs 11:3-6, 8, 10, 11, 30 ESV)

Righteous living. There are many who say and claim that Christian living and following Jesus is restrictive, legalistic, and too demanding. They say that freedom to do whatever one wants is freeing and uplifting. Not so, says the wise writer of Proverbs. It is by righteous living that people and neighbors and cities prosper and are healthy.

Righteous living keeps us walking straight and true. The repeated metaphor in Proverbs concerning righteousness and foolishness is that of a straight path versus a crooked and wayward path. A straight path is to be chosen for its ease of travel and its blessings. A wayward path is one in which people stumble and fall and are led into byways that produce death and destruction. It is a reminder of the saying, "Be sure your sins find you out." Calmness and security and even prosperity are found in walking a straight path. What kind of path are you walking?

Righteous living produces life giving joy and blessing for many. In a reminder of Psalm 1, righteous living is a tree of life — "He is like a tree planted by streams of water that yields its fruit in its season, and its leaf does not wither. In all that he does, he prospers." (Ps 1:3) It is not that everything always goes well for the righteous, but most everything turns out well for them. The difference is in the results of righteous living. Cities prosper, neighbors are cared for, confidences are kept and his or her desires end in good. Moreover, righteous living joined with "capturing souls" gives abundant blessing. This is the way of wisdom.

Lord God, help me in and through Christ to walk in the ways of wisdom and righteous living. Deliver me from paths that would lead me astray into darkness and death and destruction. Help me walk a straight path so that others may see and rejoice in it. For your honor and glory.

Self Reflection & Discussion
1. Do you live righteously? How do you know?
2. Why are paths of unrighteousness so crooked and wayward?
3. Have you witnessed towns and cities blessed by righteous living in their midst? How so?

The Power of Words
DAY 12

"A prudent man conceals knowledge, but the heart of fools proclaims folly. The hand of the diligent will rule, while the slothful will be put to forced labor. Anxiety in a man's heart weighs him down, but a good word makes him glad. One who is righteous is a guide to his neighbor, but the way of the wicked leads them astray. . . .In the path of righteousness is life, and in its pathway there is no death."
(Proverbs 12: 23-26, 28 ESV)

The power of words. Have you ever thought about how your words impact those around you? The old saying, "sticks and stones may break my bones, but words can never harm me" is deceitfully false. Words can bring life, joy, healing and needed knowledge, or they can ruin, harm and destroy. Many of the Proverbs talk about the power of words. Note what Proverbs 12 says about the power of words.

Truthful words bring justice and healing — "Whoever speaks the truth gives honest evidence, but a false witness utters deceit. There is one whose rash words are like sword thrusts, but the tongue of the wise brings healing. Truthful lips endure forever, but a lying tongue is but for a moment." (Proverbs 12:17-19) Truthful words are helpful to those weighed down by anxiety and worry. Truthful words lead to life here and now and for all eternity. "From the fruit of his mouth a man is satisfied with good, and the work of a man's hand comes back to him." (Proverbs 12:14) How often I have seen truthful words give needed hope and healing to tortured souls!

Lying words deceive and finally destroy the hearer — "The thoughts of the righteous are just; the counsels of the wicked are deceitful. The words of the wicked lie in wait for blood, but the mouth of the upright delivers them. . . . An evil man is ensnared by the transgression of his lips, but the righteous escapes from trouble. . . . There is one whose rash words are like sword thrusts, but the tongue of the wise brings healing." (Proverbs 12:5,6,13,18) These words are usually hastily spoken, rash words without thought or consideration for the hearer. They act as "sword thrusts," injuring or killing the hearer. The power of words. Be careful what you say and how it is said.

Lord God, help my words this day bring hope and health and truth to a world captivated by lies and deceit. Make my words a salve to those weighed down by anxiety and worry. Help me guard my words and think before I speak. For your honor and glory and the good of others.

Self Reflection & Discussion
1. Read Ephesians 4:29 – 5:4 on the power of words. What do you learn from these verses in conjunction with Proverbs 12?
2. Have you experienced hurtful words? Helpful words? Truthful words?
3. Review your words in the last few months. Have they been truthful and helpful? How so?

True Wealth

DAY 13

"The soul of the sluggard craves and gets nothing, while the soul of the diligent is richly supplied. . . . One pretends to be rich, yet has nothing; another pretends to be poor, yet has great wealth. . . . Wealth gained hastily will dwindle, but whoever gathers little by little will increase it. . . . Poverty and disgrace come to him who ignores instruction, but whoever heeds reproof is honored. . . .A good man leaves an inheritance to his children's children, but the sinner's wealth is laid up for the righteous."
(Proverbs 13:4, 7, 11, 18, 22 ESV)

True wealth. One of the blessings of those who live righteous lives is the gaining and disposal of wealth. And, while we may think of ourselves as not very wealthy at all, in the eyes and reality of the world, Americans are quite well to do. What are some of the markers of true wealth?

True wealth comes from honest and hard work. Building oneself up "from his bootstraps" is an old but rather true picture of wealth gained from hard work, long hours and persistence. While socialists decry capitalism, that economic process has allowed many people to gain and secure wealth. The point here is that true wealth, wealth that one can fruitfully use and enjoy, comes from diligence in one's profession under God.

True wealth is not flaunted wealth. Those truly wealthy do not pretend to be wealthy. Prideful gaining of wealth may get a person the money, but not the honor of being wealthy according to Proverbs. Humility is always to be sought in the gaining and using of wealth.

True wealth is not instant riches. Those who win lotteries and games and gain wealth through gambling are not possessors of true wealth. In fact, many who get rich quickly spend it all rather quickly and foolishly. They have not learned the secret of true wealth gained through hard work and little by little saving and using wealth properly. Be careful of get rich quick schemes. Even if you win, that is not an indicator of true wealth in God's sight.

True wealth can be handed down. In fact, it can be handed down to your "children's children" or your grandchildren. Wealth gained from following God and his ways lasts through generations. Wealth gained from foolish habits and sinful ways will perish with the death of the person. This is an interesting observation from Solomon, given that his wealth never did last for the nation or his successor. What we leave our kids and grandkids can be true security if it has been gained through true wealth.

Lord God, thank You for the provisions You have granted to us. Help us use those provisions wisely and fruitfully and humbly for your honor and glory. Help those of us who are younger and building what we call "nest eggs" do so biblically and wisely. For your honor and glory.

Self Reflection & Discussion
1. Would you say you are "wealthy?" Why or why not?
2. Define "wealth" and "poverty" from a biblical point of view.
3. Have you been the recipient of inheritances? What are some thoughts of those who left you wealth and goods?

Careful Wise Living

DAY 14

"The simple believes everything, but the prudent gives thought to his steps. One who is wise is cautious and turns away from evil, but a fool is reckless and careless. A man of quick temper acts foolishly, and a man of evil devices is hated. The simple inherit folly, but the prudent are crowned with knowledge."

(Proverbs 14:15–18 ESV)

Careful wise living. What do you do when you see "stop" and "caution" signs while driving, or when you see a backed up line of traffic? Some people get really annoyed, shout, stomp on their horns, get angry and upset and find their blood pressures and stress levels rising. Others seek a way around the mess, slow down when a caution sign is flashing and pay greater attention to where traffic is tied up. The differences between foolish people and those who live in righteous fear of the Lord are outlined in Proverbs 14.

Wise people live in caution. They are usually not risk takers or only take measured risks in work and ministry. They are careful, thoughtful and willing to pay attention to the warning signs in them and around them. They are prudent. I like that word. It means wise or judicious in practical affairs, sagacious, discreet or circumspect, sober and careful in providing for the future, provident. Wise people in God's sight look out for signs of trouble to avoid it and to take another way. They are not hasty in their decisions and life choices. When they rule in any capacity, people rejoice and feel safe and comforted. Are you a cautious and wise person?

Wise people have a settled heart in the Lord — "Whoever is slow to anger has great understanding, but he who has a hasty temper exalts folly. A tranquil heart gives life to the flesh, but envy makes the bones rot." (Proverbs 14:29, 30) They seek to avoid the stress that kills too many in our day. They live with a focused gaze on their Lord and seek a heart and inner life that is stable and requisite for the times in which they live. They live with understanding and focus. Their routines breath confidence and steadiness to those around them. Is this your life in the Lord?

Lord God, grant me a steady and stable inner life. Help me live with focus and prudence. Help me cherish the fear of You and seek to be cautious and circumspect in everything I say and do and think. For your honor and glory.

Self Reflection & Discussion
1. Are you a cautious and wise person, or are you a risk taker?
2. The modern world applauds risk takers, and young people are urged to take risks and make something of themselves. How would this chapter in Proverbs advise them?
3. How have you seen stability in those you admire?

Under God

DAY 15

"The eyes of the LORD are in every place, keeping watch on the evil and the good... The sacrifice of the wicked is an abomination to the LORD, but the prayer of the upright is acceptable to him.... Sheol and Abaddon lie open before the LORD; how much more the hearts of the children of man!...The LORD tears down the house of the proud but maintains the widow's boundaries. The thoughts of the wicked are an abomination to the LORD, but gracious words are pure."
(Proverbs 15:3, 8, 11, 25, 26 ESV)

Under God. We used to freely say in this country that we are "under God." That declaration and confession has lost its place in many quarters. "So help me God" is often not said in court hearings. We don't swear on the Bible anymore. We are adrift and I believe are paying the price for such waywardness. Proverbs 15 brings us back to being "under God." What does that actually mean?

It means that God sees and knows everything we do, say and think. Nothing is out of bounds for Him and nothing escapes his penetrating knowledge and gaze. To just know that everything we are and do and feel and think are "under God" is a blessing to those who walk in the way of wisdom and the fear of the Lord. To others, it spells judgment, lack of hearing one's prayers and final destruction. We resist such sovereign oversight, yet that is our lot in this life and on this earth. We are all "under God."

It means that eternal life and eternal death is governed by the Lord, not us. The place of the dead (*Sheol*) and the realm of the Devil (*Abaddon*) are under God's sovereign control and dictates. God knows the thoughts of the proud in heart and sees the thoughts of the wicked. This divine scrutiny and knowledge is inescapable. We are to therefore watch our tongues, order our steps and sanctify our worship of Him who knows and sees and governs everything. We all have everyday choices to make, either to recognize they are all under God or to deny God and go our own way. Proverbs 15 is a clarion call to watch, heed, listen and live in the fear of the Lord and thus walk in wisdom.

Thank You, dear Lord, that we are all under Your sovereign and perfect and loving control and sovereign direction. Help me this day not merely affirm this but live out this reality in my own life and thoughts and words and deeds. For your honor and glory.

Self Reflection & Discussion
1. What does "under God" mean to you practically day by day?
2. Does God's sovereign rule encourage or defeat your choices?
3. If everything is truly "under God," what about the evil in this world?

God and Man

DAY 16

"The plans of the heart belong to man, but the answer of the tongue is from the LORD. All the ways of a man are pure in his own eyes, but the LORD weighs the spirit. Commit your work to the LORD, and your plans will be established. The LORD has made everything for its purpose, even the wicked for the day of trouble. . . .The heart of man plans his way, but the LORD establishes his steps. . . There is a way that seems right to a man, but its end is the way to death. . . The lot is cast into the lap, but its every decision is from the LORD."

(Proverbs 16:1-4, 9, 25, 33 ESV)

God and man. The Apostle Paul notes — "Therefore, my beloved, as you have always obeyed, so now, not only as in my presence but much more in my absence, work out your own salvation with fear and trembling, for it is God who works in you, both to will and to work for his good pleasure." (Philippians 2:12, 13) There Is work for people to do for God, but it is God who is working in us to accomplish his sovereign will. This is a both/and truth and declaration.

We must plan and do. This may seem apparent to everyone, but it is necessary to understand what God is saying in Proverbs 16. We do not get away with "Let go and let God." Rather it is "Get going with God." There are some Christians who incorrectly believe and think that we have little to do with what God wants of us. It is this incorrect passiveness that prevents God's people from doing all they can to accomplish what God wants of them. God wants us to choose righteousness and do righteous and just deeds, and WE must step out in faith and trust and do them. An example would be praying for what God has told us He wants done. It may sound pious to say, "let thy will be done" but when it is biblically obvious what God's will is, to pray this way is pointless and demeaning to God. We just need to get busy and do what God wants, not wait for some sign or voice or nudge from heaven to do so.

God is behind everything. Even the wicked for the day of trouble. The sovereign and perfect God finally determines what plans we make and do succeed and what plans do not. God is still on the throne, still accomplishing his perfect and immutable will. People have problems with this, supposing that either we have unrestrained freedom of the will or that we are merely puppets under God's thumb. Both ends of the spectrum are false. As we seek to do what God wants of us, He is working in us to accomplish his eternal purposes. The Bible everywhere paints this both/and picture.

O Lord, help me this day do what I need and must accomplish for you. Help me as I work and plan and do to realize that nothing happens apart from your glorious sovereign will and declarations. Deliver me from not doing when I should be doing, and not trusting when I must just trust You for all outcomes. For your honor and glory.

Self Reflection & Discussion

1. Do you agree that the Bible paints a both/and picture of human will and sovereignty of God? How have you seen this demonstrated in your own life choices?
2. What does it mean to you that "God is behind everything?"
3. Why do we go to extremes in discussing God's overall control and rule and our human freedom?

The Fool

DAY 17

"An evildoer listens to wicked lips, and a liar gives ear to a mischievous tongue. Fine speech is not becoming to a fool; still less is false speech to a prince. A rebuke goes deeper into a man of understanding than a hundred blows into a fool. Let a man meet a she-bear robbed of her cubs rather than a fool in his folly. Why should a fool have money in his hand to buy wisdom when he has no sense? He who sires a fool gets himself sorrow, and the father of a fool has no joy. The discerning sets his face toward wisdom, but the eyes of a fool are on the ends of the earth. A foolish son is a grief to his father and bitterness to her who bore him."
(Proverbs 17:4, 7, 10, 12, 16, 21, 24-25 ESV)

The fool. The book of Proverbs has quite a lot to say about a "fool." Here "fool" means a morally corrupt and senseless person without God as the guide of his life, words, thoughts and actions. To fully understand how to live for God we also need to understand the opposite lifestyle.

A fool brings shame and reproach to his or her parents. Perhaps one of the most difficult cases in pastoral counseling or counseling in general is how to deal with parents who have raised a foolish son or daughter. While sometimes how a son or daughter turns out is the fault of bad parenting, often it is not so easy to delineate. Foolishness resides deep in the heart of a person, and the rejection of God in their lives condemns them to foolish thoughts, foolish acts and a foolish life. Sometimes we can spot a foolish son or daughter, but many times their rejection of the Lord makes them foolish. We therefore need to pray for and teach and model godliness before our kids.

A fool does not know how to deal with rebuke. Actually, rebuke makes them worse off than better. The folly of a fool prevents them from taking a godly rebuke to heart. Often they will turn a rebuke into a weapon against you. The point is that only God in his infinite mercy and grace can conquer and change the heart, mind and desires of a foolish man or woman. Only God can penetrate the heart. We all know this truth, but sometimes we want a change to come because of our efforts. Again, the solution to foolish behavior is a change of heart and attitude which comes only from the favor of God. This is why we don't waste time arguing with foolish people but rather commit them to God's mercy and intervention.

Lord God, teach me how to interact with foolish people who have turned away from You. Help me pray harder, and deal more wisely with these kinds of people. Intervene with your great mercy and transforming grace in the lives of the foolish ones around me. For your Name's sake.

Self Reflection & Discussion

1. Do you know foolish people? How do you think they got that way?
2. How would you counsel or advise parents of children who go their foolish ways?
3. Why should we not waste time in discussing important topics with a foolish person?

The Fruit of One's Mouth

DAY 18

"A brother offended is more unyielding than a strong city, and quarreling is like the bars of a castle. From the fruit of a man's mouth his stomach is satisfied; he is satisfied by the yield of his lips. Death and life are in the power of the tongue, and those who love it will eat its fruits."
(Proverbs 18:19-21 ESV)

The fruit of one's mouth. Again in Proverbs 18 we find wise advice concerning how to speak, when to listen, and what to say when. If we paid more attention to such wisdom we would have fewer relationship break-ups and quarrels and misgivings. We therefore need to listen to wisdom's advice and instructions here.

The tongue is powerful. Much of what we say evidences who we really are. In fact, death and life are in its powerful outbursts. Offense given and taken are likened to a fortified city and the bars of a castle. You cannot take back what you have said. You can apologize for it perhaps, but like used toothpaste it cannot be put back into the tube. The advice is to think before you speak and not blabber about like a fool — "An intelligent heart acquires knowledge, and the ear of the wise seeks knowledge." (V. 15) "If one gives an answer before he hears, it is his folly and shame." (V. 13)

Words are like "deep waters" — "The words of a man's mouth are deep waters; the fountain of wisdom is a bubbling brook.." (V. 4) Blurting out words without thought and consideration can cause much harm and grief. What you say often reveals who you are. Under cross examination, one can find truth in a person's words — "The one who states his case first seems right, until the other comes and examines him." (V. 17) Safety and wisdom are found by honoring and fleeing to the Lord and his strong Name — "The name of the LORD is a strong tower; the righteous man runs into it and is safe." (V. 10) Practice listening today rather than speaking right away. That is the hidden wisdom of Proverbs 18.

Lord God, guard what I say, when I say it and to whom today. Help me think before I speak and realize that my words can either heal or destroy another person. Help me always run to You, my Strong Tower. For your Name's sake.

Self Reflection & Discussion

1. Have you found your words "powerful?" How so?
2. Can you think of a time when you wish you would not have said what you said? What has been the result of such words?
3. Has anyone ever come to you hurt by the words you have expressed? How have you handled that meeting?

Common Sense Living

DAY 19

"Listen to advice and accept instruction, that you may gain wisdom in the future. Many are the plans in the mind of a man, but it is the purpose of the LORD that will stand. What is desired in a man is steadfast love, and a poor man is better than a liar. The fear of the LORD leads to life, and whoever has it rests satisfied; he will not be visited by harm."
(Proverbs 19:20–23 ESV)

Common sense living. What is "common sense?" It is that sense about life and things that allows a person freedom from taking unnecessary risks and foolish ways. It is that day-to-day, moment-by-moment practical wisdom about how life should work and what to do and what not to do. Proverbs 19 is filled with common sense standards for everybody. Let's listen to them.

"Better is a poor person who walks in his integrity than one who is crooked in speech and is a fool. Desire without knowledge is not good, and whoever makes haste with his feet misses his way." (Vv 1, 2) Walking in integrity, honest speech and desire with knowledge are common sense ways to live. That is set against crooked speech and hasty actions without knowledge. Too often our sinful tendency is to react rather than respond to situations. We jump into something without thinking and without knowing about it. Common sense living under God is honest speech and informed actions.

"Whoever gets sense loves his own soul; he who keeps understanding will discover good." (V. 8) Loving who you really are demands common sense and keeping understanding. People who try to deny who God made them to be and do are foolish and unwise. They go against the image of God implanted in the core of their being. That image, under Christ, is being renewed day by day in goodness, righteousness and true knowledge

— "assuming that you have heard about him and were taught in him, as the truth is in Jesus, to put off your old self, which belongs to your former manner of life and is corrupt through deceitful desires, and to be renewed in the spirit of your minds, and to put on the new self, created after the likeness of God in true righteousness and holiness." (Ephesians 4:21-24) Common sense is part of what the "new self" relishes and follows. It is not that unsaved people have no common sense, but rather that they live a "patch quilt" life where darkness to what is good, and righteous and true is predominant. At times what is righteous and pure and true will shine through, but only at times. What God wants is "steadfast love," living in and under the fear of God.

Lord God, make me a man of common sense with understanding. Help me live a life of integrity and common sense in all things. Deliver me from crooked speech and rashness in making choices. Help me live in your fear and love. For your honor and glory.

Self Reflection & Discussion
1. Have you found your life in Christ giving you "common sense" understanding? How so?
2. Do you find you "react" or "respond" to criticism and opinions around you?
3. If a newer Christian, have you found a difference in your level of common sense? How so?

Presumptive Cheating

DAY 20

"Who can say, "I have made my heart pure; I am clean from my sin"?
Unequal weights and unequal measures are both alike an abomination
to the LORD. Even a child makes himself known by his acts, by whether
his conduct is pure and upright. The hearing ear and the seeing eye, the
LORD has made them both. Love not sleep, lest you come to poverty;
open your eyes, and you will have plenty of bread. "Bad, bad," says the
buyer, but when he goes away, then he boasts."
(Proverbs 20:9–14 ESV)

Presumptive cheating. There are two common sins that Proverbs 20 speaks of — presumption and cheating. Presumption is when we assume something without any evidence and cheating is trying to get something for nothing, or trying to secure something falsely.

Presumption leads to unprofitable laziness and claiming sinlessness before God. Consequently, lack of hard and honest work, work done on time and in season, work that God requires results in poverty and need. There are too many who assume that something can be gained from nothing, from lack of honest work and effort. People therefore play the lottery and gamble away what God has given them looking for quick and easy riches. Consumerism drives too many and they look for a quick way to collect stuff without counting the consequences and assuming that God does not see them or care what they are doing. The God who knows our hearts, who sees into the very depths of our being, cannot be presumed upon. The Bible makes clear that freedom from sin comes only through a trusting relationship with Jesus Christ and his righteousness on our behalf.

Cheating is the other sin that Proverbs 20 highlights. "Unequal weights and unequal measures" are falsifying standards that deceive people into thinking they have purchased or gained what was expected. Think of the products that we buy. Candy bars, for instance, keep going up in price and they keep getting smaller and smaller. Boxed products are at times filled with less than what they were a year beforehand, but offered at the same or a higher price. Of course, producers claim that rising costs of what makes up their products drive this trend. But the problem is deceiving the public into thinking they are buying the exact same thing they purchased some time ago, but it is not the same thing. Liquid laundry detergents are often more water than detergent, but the buyer assumes they are getting the claimed amount of detergent.

We all need to live by the standard of "buyer beware." Hourly workers who quit at 4:30 PM instead of 5:00 PM, their expected work time, are cheaters. Fifteen minute breaks extend into half hour personal business or play. We all know these practices and may even glance away when they are normally done. This is not honoring to God in keeping up a system of false weights and measures. When we claim to do everything to glorify the God who made and redeemed us, that includes getting what we pay for and working the hours for which we agreed.

Lord, again, help me live a life of integrity and trust in You for all things. Deliver me from cutting corners, or cheating in small things, or presuming upon your love and care. Help me truly honor You in whatever I do or make or sell. For your Name's sake.

Self Reflection & Discussion
1. How do you interpret "buyer beware" in your life decisions?
2. You have heard it said that "there is no free lunch." What does that mean in your daily dealings?
3. Have you experienced "false weights and measures" in purchasing? How so? What have you done about it?
4. Have you taken things home from the office or workplace without permission? Or taken longer than allowed breaks? Or quit before the work day is officially over? What does Proverbs 20 tell you about such things?

What God Wants

DAY 21

"Every way of a man is right in his own eyes, but the LORD weighs the heart. To do righteousness and justice is more acceptable to the LORD than sacrifice. . . The plans of the diligent lead surely to abundance, but everyone who is hasty comes only to poverty .... When justice is done, it is a joy to the righteous but terror to evildoers. One who wanders from the way of good sense will rest in the assembly of the dead , . . Whoever pursues righteousness and kindness will find life, righteousness, and honor. A wise man scales the city of the mighty and brings down the stronghold in which they trust. Whoever keeps his mouth and his tongue keeps himself out of trouble."
(Proverbs 21:2, 3, 5, 15, 16, 21-23 ESV)

What God wants. These verses remind me of the very famous prophetic word in Micah — "Will the LORD be pleased with thousands of rams, with ten thousands of rivers of oil? Shall I give my firstborn for my transgression, the fruit of my body for the sin of my soul?" He has told you, O man, what is good; and what does the LORD require of you but to do justice, and to love kindness, and to walk humbly with your God? (Micah 6:7, 8)

God wants righteousness and justice from us. We so love to substitute what we think God wants with what He really wants from us. In fact, we would rather go to church than BE the church in this world. We would rather offer sacrifices of praise and church work rather than doing that work for the poor and needy and oppressed. This was, after all, Israel's sin and way of placating the God of their fathers. They were religious, indeed, but failed at righteousness and justice, especially for their poor and oppressed. We are only made righteous in and through Jesus Christ, but that does not relieve us of practicing righteousness and justice with others. Are these two qualities seen in your life today? How so?

God wants kindness to the needy and neighbor around us. We need to "pursue" kindness, not exercise it as a "here and there" kind of quality or characteristic. I sometimes wonder how many Christians are seen as "kind." Right theology and trips to the homeless shelter are fine, but we are to develop a life of kindness and relief to those around us who are our neighbors and the poor of our neighborhoods. We live in a day when many restaurant workers are laboring for pennies on the dollar. If we have the resources we need to leave them healthy tips and even return the change they bring to us after a meal. I have met working mothers trying to get by on restaurant tips. This is one area where practicing kindness counts.

Lord, help me this day and in my life practice righteousness and justice and kindness to those around me, those I meet every day, those who make me my restaurant meals, collect my garbage and do those tasks I would not rather do. Help me daily show them kindness and respect and honor.
For your Name's sake.

Self Reflection & Discussion
1. Are righteousness and justice seen in your life decisions? How so?
2. Describe ways that you are kind to your neighbors.
3. Do you find the admonition of Micah 6:7, 8 practiced by your church or Christian friends? How so?

Practicing Prudence

DAY 22

"The prudent sees danger and hides himself, but the simple go on and suffer for it. The reward for humility and fear of the LORD is riches and honor and life. Thorns and snares are in the way of the crooked; whoever guards his soul will keep far from them. . . . He who loves purity of heart, and whose speech is gracious, will have the king as his friend. The eyes of the LORD keep watch over knowledge, but he overthrows the words of the traitor."

(Proverbs 22:3-5, 11, 12 ESV)

Practicing prudence. Have you ever been called a "prude?" The dictionary definition is one who is "excessively modest in speech, conduct, dress and so forth." Society looks at prudishness as a liability, as out of step with success and influence. However, Proverbs sees it quite differently. Prudence is an admirable quality and what God wants of us.

Prudence guards one's path in life. Being prudent allows us to escape upcoming danger and harm. Prudence sees what lies ahead and prepares for it. Prudence is the way of knowledge and final influence in life. Such a lifestyle and mindset goes against the worldly way of taking risks and driving toward danger, seeing how brave or how close we can come to the edge of a cliff without falling off. Prudence seeks knowledge and avoids obvious danger. And the reward for such humility and fear of God is "riches and honor and life." Indeed, as one writer says, this truth is "often, but not always." Not all prudent people get rich and honored as successful by society, but they are deemed so by God. And that is what matters.

Prudent people watch over their souls. Their inner life is of first importance. They know that if their inner life is right with God then their outer words and life will be fine. Stability inside leads to stability in the outside world. How stable is your soul? What is your inside like before God? Instead of cosmetic cures on the outside, we are to guard our hearts and secure our souls in Christ.

Prudent people have final influence. They are often sought out by those in authority and power for their "saneness," their awareness of things as they really are. They are not deceived by power plays or by climbing to the top over people. They have gracious speech and are pure in heart and life. Holiness is the badge they wear. And even though many disdain them, in the final analysis they are asked for their input and advice. Right after seminary I worked for a commercial painting outfit, pastoring a starter church. I was often called "preacher boy" by the crew and did not join them in "happy hour" after work. But when trouble came to their lives they sought me out for prayer and guidance. This is what often happens to prudent people who live in the fear of God.

O Lord, help me live a holy and prudent life before You and the world. Deliver me from danger at every turn and help me influence those around me by my prudence. Use me at every level of society for your honor and glory.
For your Name's sake.

Self Reflection & Discussion
1. Would you describe your life as a "prudent" life? How so?
2. Do you agree that prudent people have final influence? Have you seen this mirrored in your life?
3. Deal with the question — How stable is your soul?

Addiction

DAY 23

"Who has woe? Who has sorrow? Who has strife? Who has complaining?
Who has wounds without cause? Who has redness of eyes? Those who
tarry long over wine; those who go to try mixed wine. Do not look at
wine when it is red, when it sparkles in the cup and goes down smoothly.
In the end it bites like a serpent and stings like an adder. Your eyes will
see strange things, and your heart utter perverse things. You will be like
one who lies down in the midst of the sea, like one who lies on the top of
a mast. They struck me," you will say, "but I was not hurt; they beat me,
but I did not feel it. When shall I awake? I must have another drink."
(Proverbs 23:29–35 ESV)

Addiction. I heard a TV comic say last evening that there are five
stages of getting drunk, beginning at 11 PM and ending at sunrise.
Each stage is a downhill slide into oblivion and "giving in to the
devil on your shoulder." It was funny, in a tragic and frightfully honest sort
of way. And that's the problem, isn't it? People who are drunks cannot stop
their downhill slide into useless and destructive oblivion. Thus the warning
of Proverbs 23.

Addiction is a choice that becomes a raging master. The current trend
is to say that addiction to alcohol and drugs and overeating and under
eating and so forth is a disease that can be treated like any other sickness
or illness. The effects may induce sickness of mind and body, but the initial
stages of addiction are sinful choices. It is those choices that must change
for addiction to really stop. The warning of Proverbs against drunkenness
and gluttony must be taken seriously. What we want is often not what God
wants for us. And the want becomes an obsession and the obsession an
addiction.

Don't be misled into addiction of any kind. The beginning stages look
inviting and carefree. Strong wine "goes down smoothly but in the end bites

like a serpent and stings like an adder." Talk to a recovering alcoholic and he or she will affirm these stages of addiction. Most anything can become an addiction, like wanting the finest food and the wealthiest setting possible. It seems innocent enough but if this is not what God wants for you and your life, those first steps into addiction can seize and defeat you. Choose wise living in the fear of the Lord. Beware what the comic last night said about "the devil on your shoulder" urging you on. It is not funny and not real happiness and contentment.

Lord, keep me far away from addiction of any kind over anything. Help me choose wisely in your fear and love always. Help me see ahead and avoid the ravages of addiction. Deliver me from choices that lead to gut wrenching and heart wrenching paths. For your Name's sake.

Self Reflection & Discussion
1. Do you have any "addictions?" What have you done to fight them?
2. Do you agree with the comic that the "Devil made me do it?"
3. Do you agree that it is true that so often what we want from God and what God wants from us do not coincide? Why?

Living Around Sinners

DAY 24

"Be not envious of evil men, nor desire to be with them, for their hearts devise violence, and their lips talk of trouble. . .If you faint in the day of adversity, your strength is small. Rescue those who are being taken away to death; hold back those who are stumbling to the slaughter. If you say, "Behold, we did not know this," does not he who weighs the heart perceive it? Does not he who keeps watch over your soul know it, and will he not repay man according to his work? ... Fret not yourself because of evildoers, and be not envious of the wicked, for the evil man has no future; the lamp of the wicked will be put out."
(Proverbs 24;1, 2, 10-12, 19-20 ESV)

Living around sinners. How does the Christian maintain his cool around people who reject Christ and don't fear God? How then should we live around scoffers and schemers of evil and sin?

Don't copy, join with or envy them. It is sometimes a temptation to do what sinners do and be where sinners are. I am using the term "sinners" not to be holier-then-thou but rather to designate those who consistently reject God and his Word and choose to do sinful things. We are to stay away from them and their deeds. We are not to plan evil with them. We are not to do harm to our neighbor with them. They are on a pathway to eternal destruction and failure. Joining with them, even in thought and desire, places us on a similar path with them.

Don't get back at them — "Do not rejoice when your enemy falls, and let not your heart be glad when he stumbles, lest the LORD see it and be displeased, and turn away his anger from him." (Proverbs 24:17, 18) Isn't this what Jesus taught — "You have heard that it was said, 'You shall love your neighbor and hate your enemy.' But I say to you, Love your enemies and pray for those who persecute you." (Matt 5:43, 44) and what Paul advises about retaliation — "Beloved, never avenge yourselves, but leave it to the wrath of God, for it is written, "Vengeance is mine, I will repay, says the Lord." (Romans 12:19) We are not to overcome evil with evil but with God's goodness and the power of love. We are to rest secure knowing that any payback will be done by God himself in his own time and way and will.

Rescue the perishing — "Rescue those who are being taken away to death; hold back those who are stumbling to the slaughter." (Proverbs 24:11), and we recall what James said about those wandering from God — "My brothers, if anyone among you wanders from the truth and someone brings him back, let him know that whoever brings back a sinner from his wandering will save his soul from death and will cover a multitude of sins." (James 5:19, 20) We are still our brother's keeper, no matter how far they stumble and go astray. Those whom we can help, we do help. That does not mean that those running from God will heed and listen and turn around. It simply means we do all in our power to rescue them from certain judgment and destruction. We are to always live above sin and evil and scoffers and schemers.

Lord, today help me not to envy what those who reject You have and do and say. Deliver me from wanting to get back at them. Help me rather to do good to them and seek to lead those going astray from that path. Teach me to treat people like Jesus did. For his Name's sake.

Self Reflection & Discussion
1. Many of us live around those who practice a sinful lifestyle. How have they affected you?
2. How do you deal with the evil around you that personally affects you?
3. Have you had a part in "rescuing the perishing, and caring for the dying?"

All About Self-Control

DAY 25

"Do not put yourself forward in the king's presence or stand in the place of the great, for it is better to be told, "Come up here," than to be put lower in the presence of a noble. What your eyes have seen do not hastily bring into court, for what will you do in the end, when your neighbor puts you to shame? Argue your case with your neighbor himself, and do not reveal another's secret, lest he who hears you bring shame upon you, and your ill repute have no end. . . . If you have found honey, eat only enough for you, lest you have your fill of it and vomit it. Let your foot be seldom in your neighbor's house, lest he have his fill of you and hate you. . . .It is not good to eat much honey, nor is it glorious to seek one's own glory. A man without self-control is like a city broken into and left without walls."

(Proverbs 25:6–10; 16, 17, 27-28 ESV)

All about self-control. It seems that one of the hardest lessons in life is to learn the art of self-control. It is indeed so hard that Paul cites it in Galatians 5 as one of the fruits of the Spirit (Gal 5:22, 23). This clues us into what makes and Who gives self-control. While we can grow in self-control through human devices, the ultimate blessing of self-control comes from the Holy Spirit at work in our hearts and lives.

Self-control covers all aspects of life. How we appear and conduct ourselves in the presence of those above us in authority, how we deal with our neighbor's secret confessions to us as a friend, how we eat sweets and how we advance in our careers all involve the mastery of self-control. It is always better to be promoted by someone above you who notices your skills rather than self-promotion through being in the right places at the right times or heralding that we have the answers. This goes against modern "you can do it all" hogwash that even our kids hear at school and in sports or any competition. The drive to be "Number 1" rails against self-control and forces us to take unwarranted risks at the cost of others and even our own mental and spiritual health.

Self-control shores up our defenses against pride and self-congratulation. Without it we are indeed like "a city broken and left without walls." Self-control guards the gates to our ears, eyes, thoughts and hearts. Self-control tempers a hasty judgment to condemn another without knowing all the facts. Self-control helps our overweight problems with common sense in eating sweets. Self-control allows us to have self-respect and the respect and honor of others. If we had more self-control we would have less problems in the world, the church and the home. Grow in and pray for more self-control.

Lord, I ask for much more self-control than I possess. Help me grow in self-control in all things. Teach me a moderate lifestyle. Deliver me from thinking I can do anything apart from your grace and strength.
For your honor and glory.

Self Reflection & Discussion

1. Why do you think that self-control is listed as one of the fruits of the Spirit in Galatians 5?
2. These proverbs challenge us to exercise self-control, not merely with our emotions, but also our eating habits and neighborly contacts. Why is self-control important in these arenas of life?
3. When was the last time you had an opportunity to advance in your career or place in society? How did you handle that promotion?

Tattling & Quarreling
DAY 26

"For lack of wood the fire goes out, and where there is no whisperer, quarreling ceases. As charcoal to hot embers and wood to fire, so is a quarrelsome man for kindling strife. The words of a whisperer are like delicious morsels; they go down into the inner parts of the body. Like the glaze covering an earthen vessel are fervent lips with an evil heart. Whoever hates disguises himself with his lips and harbors deceit in his heart; when he speaks graciously, believe him not, for there are seven abominations in his heart; though his hatred be covered with deception, his wickedness will be exposed in the assembly."
(Proverbs 26:20-26 ESV)

Tattling and quarreling. This chapter in Proverbs unveils two common sins of humankind -- tattling, or gossiping, and quarreling. They are most likely the two most prevalent ills that have afflicted all of humankind. We need therefore to hear the words of wisdom on these matters today.

Tattling. Telling stories out of school. Revealing secrets. While they seem "delicious" in the intaking, they are evil poisons that can ruin the heart of a person. They are like a cosmetic covering to a cheap vessel or knockoff. They are the words of a foolish person who cannot keep his or her tongue. The Apostle Paul warns us about this kind of sin in these last days — "For among them are those who creep into households and capture weak women, burdened with sins and led astray by various passions, always learning and never able to arrive at a knowledge of the truth." (2 Tim 3:6, 7) Thus, the craze for daily soap operas and the vapid collection of so-called "secrets" about others, which are then shared and talked about incessantly. And they don't need to be soaps. They can be TV preachers, so called Elmer Gantry's, of today, always selling and hawking something. The advice— AVOID THEM.

Quarreling. Fighting in homes. Fighting among neighbors. Fighting on the streets. Fighting among politicians. Fighting among heads of states. This kind of bickering and quarreling breeds a continue "fire" that refuses to go out, and can result in wars, rumors of wars, divorce, even killings. Of course, such quarreling is often "disguised" as bantering or normal ways of getting business done (see our Congress for examples). The warnings of Proverbs are severe — "Whoever meddles in a quarrel not his own is like one who takes a passing dog by the ears. Like a madman who throws firebrands, arrows, and death is the man who deceives his neighbor and says, "I am only joking!" (Proverbs 26:17-19)

Such people "disguise themselves by their lips" but their hearts are far from God and his ways. Quarreling is deceitful treachery, wanting our own way, dispensing with the wisdom of others, making it a joke and otherwise uttering destruction and grief. This is not the way of Jesus. And it must be stopped. Recall and meditate on this — "Do nothing from selfish ambition or conceit, but in humility count others more significant than yourselves. Let each of you look not only to his own interests, but also to the interests of others. Have this mind among yourselves, which is yours in Christ Jesus." (Philippians 2:3-5)

O Lord, end the often tragic fighting and quarreling and tattling that goes on too much around me, even in my own church. Deliver those of us who claim your Name and your forgiveness to avoid such behavior. Sanctify our hearts, dear Lord, and make them yours. For your honor and glory and the good of my neighbors.

Self Reflection & Discussion

1. Why do people gravitate toward gossip and quarreling?
2. How can you stop your own penchant for tattling?
3. We are to avoid gossipers, increasingly so in these "last days." Do you studiously avoid such people?

Friendship

DAY 27

"Let another praise you, and not your own mouth; a stranger, and not your own lips. . . Better is open rebuke than hidden love. Faithful are the wounds of a friend; profuse are the kisses of an enemy. . . .Oil and perfume make the heart glad, and the sweetness of a friend comes from his earnest counsel. Do not forsake your friend and your father's friend, and do not go to your brother's house in the day of your calamity. Better is a neighbor who is near than a brother who is far away."
(Proverbs 27:1, 2, 5, 6, 9, 10 ESV)

Friendship. My iWatch tells me to begin this day by reflection. Interesting that even Apple recognizes that a moment of early reflection helps the day go better. And then it tells me before I go to bed to reflect again. Friendship is one of those truths from God on which we should reflect day after day. Who in your life can you call "your friend?" And why so? Proverbs 27 gives us some thoughts.

True friends are honest with you. The truth is that we savor dishonesty about ourselves! That's right. We want people to praise us, to want to be with us, to overlook our faults and foibles, our sins and dark sides. But that is never true friendship. True friends are our reflection of who we really are to the world around us. They see us for who we really are, not who we pretend or even want to be. Their piercing wounds at times are ointment to our hearts and souls. Their words of rebuke and advice and plainly saying "no" to us are more helpful than the superficial praises of many. How often have you reflected on your true friends and noted their honest counsel with you? Without them you and I would be lost in fairyland or worse.

True friends can be neighbors. We live in a neighborhood and God has given us a few neighbors as true friends, especially the guy to our left facing the street on which we live. He is a Christian man, single and an optometrist. He has lived there a bit longer than our 14 years in this place. We have been in each other's home, cared for each other's places while away, and warned us about garage doors being left up as we forgot to close them in the morning or on a trip. We have eaten together. He was recently ill with Covid, and we checked in on him, making sure he was okay and healing up. We can count on him. We also have family not too far away, but he would be one of the first people we would call in a jam or an emergency. Do you have a neighbor who is a true friend? If not, seek to make one!

Lord, thank you for true friends, for our true friends today. I praise you for Rob, our friendly neighbor, always there for us. I thank you for others down the street that we are getting to know. I especially thank you for my accountability partner and my fellow mentor friend who have been with me through thick and thin. Bless them and their families today.
For your Name's sake.

Self Reflection & Discussion

1. Who in your life can you call your "friend" from the perspective of Proverbs 27?
2. Do you have a regular "accountability partner" with whom you discuss your deepest thoughts and feelings? If not, why not?
3. Is your neighbor your "friend?"

Justice & Integrity

DAY 28

"Those who forsake the law praise the wicked, but those who keep the law strive against them. Evil men do not understand justice, but those who seek the LORD understand it completely. Better is a poor man who walks in his integrity than a rich man who is crooked in his ways. The one who keeps the law is a son with understanding, but a companion of gluttons shames his father. . . If one turns away his ear from hearing the law, even his prayer is an abomination. Whoever misleads the upright into an evil way will fall into his own pit, but the blameless will have a goodly inheritance."

(Proverbs 28:4-7, 9, 10 ESV)

Justice and integrity. These two qualities are often sadly missing today in our politically correct world. We want fairness on our own terms, apart from any kind of God-ward reference. Keeping God's law is crucial to justice and integrity. While such keeping will not earn heaven, (only the grace of God in and through Jesus Christ will do that) it will give glory to a land and a people.

Justice and integrity are religious matters. They are tied to and allied with the fear of God and walking in his ways — "Blessed is the one who fears the LORD always, but whoever hardens his heart will fall into calamity." (V. 14) Those who walk with God are able to keep God's laws and produce righteous judgments. This is simply the evidence or outcome of salvation through Christ — "For by grace you have been saved through faith. And this is not your own doing; it is the gift of God, not a result of works, so that no one may boast. For we are his workmanship, created in Christ Jesus for good works, which God prepared beforehand, that we should walk in them." (Ephesians 2:8-10) The fear of the Lord is not merely the beginning of knowledge and wisdom. It is also the path of knowledge and wisdom and righteousness and justice for all.

Unjust and evil rulers are a curse and heartache to the people — "If one turns away his ear from hearing the law, even his prayer is an abomination. . . . When the righteous triumph, there is great glory, but when the wicked rise, people hide themselves.. . .Like a roaring lion or a charging bear is a wicked ruler over a poor people. A ruler who lacks understanding is a cruel oppressor, but he who hates unjust gain will prolong his days." (Vv 9, 12, 15, 16) What do people do under injustice? They "hide themselves." They retreat into the shadows and seek consolation elsewhere. Isn't this what has happened in many lands where injustice and tyranny are rampant? Christians often go underground in such circumstances. Not that they give up their faith, but truth and righteous judgments die in the land. These words of Solomon are often unheeded today even in our political and social climate. We need to take warning from such wisdom.

Lord, I pray for our rulers and those in authority over us. Help them to be and become godly people who keep your Word and seek your truth always for us, the people of the land. Deliver us from hiding away because of top level wickedness and injustice. For your honor and glory.

Self Reflection & Discussion
1. Do you agree that justice and integrity come from the fear of God?
2. How have you seen injustice create angst and destructive influences?
3. Pray for those "hiding" Christians who live in openly oppressive lands and states.

Two Things

DAY 30

"Two things I ask of you; deny them not to me before I die: Remove far from me falsehood and lying; give me neither poverty nor riches; feed me with the food that is needful for me, lest I be full and deny you and say, "Who is the LORD?" or lest I be poor and steal and profane the name of my God."

(Proverbs 30:7–9 ESV)

Two things. Solomon was not the only wise man in Israel and surrounding nations. 1 Kings 4:30, 31 mentions other wise people, giving Solomon as the wisest of all. Here humble Agur surveys life around him and makes a number of observations about wise living. I choose Agur's "two things" on which to comment today.

"Remove from me falsehood and lying." One of the greatest and wisest gifts we can have in life is integrity. People who live in integrity generally have trouble free lives, not always looking behind to see if what they did and said and held to was honest and fair and godly. They leave behind themselves a "wake" where others can live in safety and confidence. Lincoln's "honesty is the best policy" comes from biblical sayings such as these. People who lie and who live a lie are always seeking the better lie, the more clever lie, the one lie that will clear their consciences and set them free from inward pain. Of course, they can never find such a course of life because it is encased in lies.

"Give me neither poverty or riches." There is much wisdom in such a request. Too much money and things give the burden of worry and fretting that enough is never enough and the attempts to keep what you have consume your thoughts. Too little money leaves one open to stealing or conniving to survive. Their days become days of mere survival. People who live from paycheck to paycheck, who don't know whether they will have employment tomorrow or next week live in the throes of poverty or one step above poverty. I should know since I grew up with a father who could never keep a job and every Friday was an anxious test to see if he lost another job once again. The point is to have enough. To have as Jesus taught us to pray, "our daily bread."

Lord God, grant these two things for my life. Help me live in full trust and obedience to You. Help me always speak the truth and have just enough not to worry and fret or anxiously guard and keep what I have. May You be honored and glorified in my life always.

Self Reflection & Discussion

1. When you pray to the Lord for your "daily bread," for what are you praying?
2. Do you have "enough?" If not, or you feel that there is always more to have, consider these sayings here in Proverbs 30. I also recommend you purchase and read Michael Yankoski's *The Sacred Year* for when "enough" is really enough.
3. Do you lie? Do you find yourself creating more lies than you can possibly cover? One of the group mandates from John Wesley when he began his Methodist groups was to ask this question, rather severely I suspect.

Who To Put In Office

DAY 31A

"It is not for kings, O Lemuel, it is not for kings to drink wine, or for rulers to take strong drink, lest they drink and forget what has been decreed and pervert the rights of all the afflicted... Open your mouth for the mute, for the rights of all who are destitute. Open your mouth, judge righteously, defend the rights of the poor and needy."
(Proverbs 31:4, 5, 8, 9 ESV)

Who to put in office, that is, political office. I get a regular briefing of two parties at election time—Republican and Democrat. Sometimes I get notices of Independents who are running for office. What strikes me, and I am sure strikes you as well, is the vitriol and mud-slinging that takes place between Parties and platforms. At times, it gets ugly and abusive. The Bible makes clear what kinds of officials we should have and what should be their priorities and platforms. Two things stand out to me in these verses today.

Self-control. Whomever we place in office, that person needs to be a person of self-control and moderation. The issue here, as today, is the consumption of alcohol and the plague of drunkenness which darkens the understanding and judgment of a person. A drunk does not make a good official. Perhaps that is obvious, but it not always obvious what drunkenness looks like in different people. The "rights of the afflicted" need guarded always. That is one of the main jobs of our officials. Are your officials doing that for your community?

Judging righteously. Defending the cause of the oppressed. This is what good kings and good officials do in office. They are concerned about the down-and-out. They pass legislation and make sure the poor and needy are cared for and helped. Whether they be Democrats or Republicans or Independents, they are charged by God with a mandate to judge righteously and defend those who cannot defend themselves. This should be their platform and their "main thing." Too often, officials rule for self-interest or the concerns of the wealthy and rich lobbyists. This is not biblical rulership. Next election, look for these biblical qualities.

Thank You, Lord, for outlining what good rulers are and do. Thank You for the character qualities and positions of righteous rulers and officials. I pray today for our rulers and officials that You would convict and convince them of your requirements for their jobs. Make them a blessing and not a curse to their constituents. For your honor and glory.

Self Reflection & Discussion
1. Are your local, state and government officials defending and promoting the "rights of the afflicted" and oppressed? How so?
2. What do you look for when you are electing officials at any and all levels?
3. Do you know how to spot a drunk official?

The Godly Wife and Mother

DAY 31B

"Her husband is known in the gates when he sits among the elders of the land. She makes linen garments and sells them; she delivers sashes to the merchant. Strength and dignity are her clothing, and she laughs at the time to come. She opens her mouth with wisdom, and the teaching of kindness is on her tongue. She looks well to the ways of her household and does not eat the bread of idleness. Her children rise up and call her blessed; her husband also, and he praises her."
(Proverbs 31:23–28 ESV)

The godly wife and mother. There is perhaps no other passage in the Bible that is so often quoted on Mother's Day but so often despised by a secular world far from God. For those apart from God and his Word, this passage seems to put down women and makes them slavish to the whims of men. For those who love God and his truth, this passage resonates with those qualities that constitute a godly and reliable wife and mother.

She fulfills her creation role. Eve was created for Adam by God to "complete" or "fulfill" her husband. She was never created as "second best," or "below" the status of Adam. It is the ancient lie of the Devil, imbibed by generations of ungodliness that women are somehow "inferior" to men or slaves to their husbands. From God's point of view, a godly wife and mother is caring, resourceful, committed to her family and diligent in her responsibilities and roles. To absent women from such roles defies God and flies in the face of their creation roles. An equal status with men does not mean equal roles, but rather "shared" roles and responsibilities.

She earns the respect of her husband, her children and leaders around her in the marketplace. Her gifts and energy are legendary. Actually, many Christian women read this account and claim that it is too ideal, too "perfect" for them to ever begin to fulfill. But the truth is that a godly wife and mother most always fulfills this role and place in the home and society, even if she does not recognize it. My wife is a godly wife and mother and this passage reflects her strengths and cares and concerns. I am certain that many of those reading this devotional, if married, can attest to this description in their own wives and mothers. She deserves the praise and adoration.

Lord God, thank you for godly wives and mothers. They have been and are a blessing and bedrock of the creation You planned and envisioned. Bless them today with your presence, your power and your love. Help them continue to fulfill their God-given roles with joy and love. For your Name's sake.

Self Reflection & Discussion
1. If you are married, can you attest to this description of a godly woman as your wife? Why or why not?
2. Too often our society makes a distinction between a "stay-at-home" mom and a career woman. This passage speaks against such a distinction. Are you a career woman seeking also to be a good wife and mother? How do you balance the two?
3. How does your church celebrate "Mother's Day?"

Valuable Works on Proverbs
Selected Titles

There are a myriad of titles and books and lessons available on Proverbs. These are my recommendations for serious students of Proverbs who want to grow deeper in the Word and practice of godly living.

Charles Bridges, *Proverbs* (Geneva Series of Commentaries) (Banner of Truth Pub., Reprinted from the 1846 original publication)

Timothy Keller, *God's Wisdom for Navigating Life: A Year of Daily Devotions in the Book of Proverbs* (Viking, 2017).

Derek Kidner, *Proverbs: An Introduction and Commentary* (Tyndale Series, 1964).

Joyce Meyer, *In Search of Wisdom: Life-Changing Truths in the Book of Proverbs* (FaithWords, 2021).

Eugene Petersen, *The Message of Proverbs* (NavPress, 2016).

Charles Swindoll, *Living the Proverbs: Insight for the Daily Grind* (Worthy Publishing, 2021).

Bruce Waitke, *The Book Of Proverbs: Chapters 1-15*. (New International Commentary on the Old Testament) (Eerdmans, 2004).

Warren Wiersbe, *Be Skillful (Proverbs): God's Guidebook to Wise Living* (The BE Series Commentary) (David C. Cook, 2009).

Other Titles
by the Author

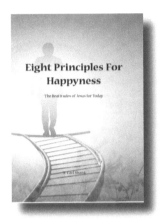

Eight Principles for Happyness: The Beatitudes of Jesus For Today, 2019.

People in Jesus are happy when they are at the end of their rope, when they feel they've lost what is most dear to them only to be embraced by the One most dear to them, when they are content with just who they are, when they have a good appetite for God, when they care, when they get their inside world put right, when they show people how to cooperate instead of compete and fight, when their commitment to God provokes persecution, and when people put them down or throw them out or speak lies about them to discredit them. (Matthew 5:3–11 The Message) Jesus understands fully the negatives in life, but his concern in these eight ethical lessons is to cheer us and tell us what real, lasting and genuine happiness is all about. That is the approach of this study of the beatitudes. (*Happyness is not a misspelling but intentional.)

Available from lulu.com and amazon.com and other booksellers.

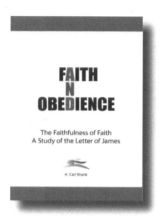

Faith and Obedience: The Faithfulness of Faith A Study of the Letter of James 2020.

In my own pastoral experience I have found the interplay of faith and obedience necessary to a true profession or confession of faith. Too often and sadly in too many cases, I have dealt with people making statements of belief in Jesus without the life to back up those statements and affirmations. I have grown weary of too many people, having been raised in Christian homes and Christian churches, lacking a heart and hands love for God in their daily habits and perspectives.

James is a needed refresher course for all those who say they believe and follow Jesus. It is a powerful message linking our day to day confession with the requirements of full obedience to Jesus Christ as Lord and Master of all.

Available from lulu.com and amazon.com and other booksellers.

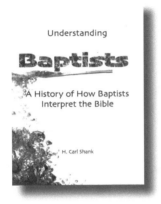

Understanding

Baptists

A History of How Baptists
Interpret the Bible

H. Carl Shank

Understanding Baptists: A History of How Baptists Interpret the Bible, 2020.

Baptist history is a tapestry of struggling with the predominant theologies of their times, a struggle that often found them either dying at the end of a stake for the cause of Christ, or railing against the prevailing interpretation of the Bible of their period in time and space and history. In this ebb and flow of history and theology, there were seasons where Baptists sought to make theological peace with other Protestants around them.

However, most of the time they found themselves struggling with the prevailing views and hermeneutical interpretations of initiation in the Church of Jesus Christ. The when, where and how of baptism, the place of children in the church, the order and life of the church and how they integrated with other believers frame much of their rich and varied history.

Available from lulu.com and amazon.com and other booksellers.

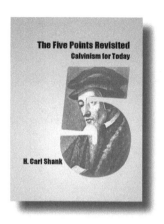

The Five Points Revisited: Calvinism for Today, 2011.

This is not an exhaustive book, nor a polemic against my Arminian friends. Nor is this a treatise on systematic theology, though there are many theological points in it. It is rather a personal restating of truths that God has impressed on my heart and mind since my college years. Rather than being weakened by all the different ministries and situations in which I have served, they have been strengthened, deepened and made more real for me by a continual study of God's Word and interactions with many Christians from a variety of theological backgrounds.

Available from lulu.com and amazon.com and other booksellers.

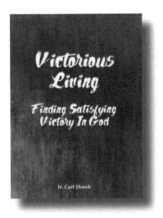

Victorious Living: Finding Satisfying Victory in God, 2020.

I am more and more convinced that many well-intentioned Christians live far below their promises from God or presume upon God for too much of the "good life," whatever that may mean. We want to live on the "mountain top" of God's favor, but too often find ourselves in the valley of trouble and outright despair. We have to learn how to live victoriously in the valleys of life with God. I believe this is not only possible, but should be the Christian "normal" for those wishing to live Christ-centered lives.

Available from lulu.com and amazon.com and other booksellers.

God This Really Hurts! Another Look at Affliction Through Job and Paul, 2021.

Too many people want a "word" of comfort from God. They want to feel better. They believe God owes it to us, as a kind heavenly Father. Consequently, we do not read nor can we understand the record of Job in the Bible. We avoid the harshness of affliction experienced by many of our forefathers of the faith.

We need a theology of comfort, not merely a list of "how to's" but a thought out, God given, time tested and biblically based understanding about comfort irrespective of the situations we face or can face. This book seeks to help us get to that well-worn, but often forgotten, perspective.

Available from lulu.com and amazon.com and other booksellers.

Winning Others for God: Effective Gospel Sharing, 2018.

I must admit that for me, next to biblical preaching and teaching of the Word of God, is reaching others for Jesus Christ. This deep passion and desire has been birthed in me, no doubt, by my father who passed away when I was in college. One of his final sayings to me was, "Son, I know what I must do to be saved, but I am not ready for that." He passed away a few months later.

Many scholars and theologians and pastors and teachers have sought to deal with the issue of effective gospel witness or biblical evangelism. Perhaps this is just one more attempt to do the same. Have we really followed Jesus in the realm of reaching others for Jesus? That is the question that drives this new book for effective evangelism in our day.

Available from lulu.com and amazon.com and other booksellers.

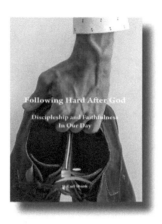

Following Hard After God: Discipleship and Faithfulness in Our Day, 2018.

Faithfulness is hard to find in anyone or anything today. It is an "older" term, a word that seems risk-aversive and not very creative. People claim that it blunts thrilling, excitement filled living and that top success in business or ministry cannot be found with it. We admire faithfulness at a distance, just so it is not the first thing that describes us and our faith journey. Notice how many people, knowing that danger is ahead on the road, go forward rather than turning around and finding another way to their destination. People race in their cars to get to a place, and pass me at unsafe speeds, only for me to catch up to them at the next stop light. Faithfulness is at a premium today.

Available from lulu.com and amazon.com and other booksellers.

Arguing for God: A Monograph on Logic and the Christian Faith, 2018.

It is often and mistakenly thought that the Christian faith, or belief in God, has nothing whatever to do with logic and rationality. Those who take such a position have been distracted by unbelievers with what they have called "logical" or "rational" arguments against faith topics, such as the existence of God, the deity and resurrection of Jesus Christ and the inspiration of the Bible. Consequently, such believers have totally divorced Christianity from rational argumentation, regarding that as a secular attack, and have championed an anti-intellectual faith stance as the only true biblical position. Many other believers, however, have noted that the Christian faith is not deism, but a faith that can be rationally taught and defended against the arguments of unbelievers.

Available from lulu.com and amazon.com and other booksellers.

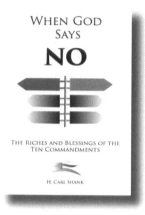

When God Says No: The Riches and Blessings of the Ten Commandments, 2019.

Our forefathers of the faith saw in the Ten Commandments God's road map for living the Christian life. While they don't repair the human heart or transform the human soul, they are God-given, explicit and undeniable tenets of how God wants us to behave in his creation toward him and toward our neighbors. Jesus never dismissed or voided the Ten Commandments. Instead, he restated them and gave them new life and vitality that the religious leaders of his day had enervated by legalistic additions and summaries.

When God Says No is a theological and practical study of the Ten Commandments. It will immerse you in what God considers right and proper behavior and will expand your horizons in almost every field of endeavor.

Available from lulu.com and amazon.com and other booksellers.

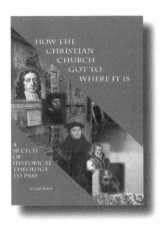

How The Christian Church Got to Where It Is: A Sketch of Historical Theology to 1900, 2018.

J. G. Vos says we study the history of doctrine because we can unduly romanticize the past. We can give it an ideal quality or character that it does not have nor deserves. There is also the problem of absolutizing the past, seizing upon one period of time as normative and ideal for all future time. Luther and the Protestant Reformers were brave souls in their time, yet their admixture of state and church led to mass persecutions of those who did not agree with town fathers. We can also disdain the past, and trash it along with valid and helpful church councils, creeds and discussions. This book takes a "slice" of church history up to 1900 and examines how we got to where we are today.

Available from lulu.com and amazon.com and other booksellers.

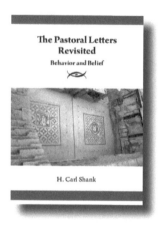

The Pastoral Letters Revisited: Behavior and Belief, 2018.

The three New Testament letters, 1 Timothy, 2 Timothy and Titus, are what we call the Pastoral Epistles. Timothy and Titus were young, energetic, trustworthy and effective as Christian workers and leaders. They were both called to difficult and challenging situations. Timothy was more shy than Titus, but both needed encouragement and instruction as how to handle false teachers and difficult questions of pastoral conduct and leadership.

This book is not an exhaustive commentary or study on the Pastoral Epistles. It is rather a close look at some of the major themes of these letters.

Available from lulu.com and amazon.com and other booksellers.

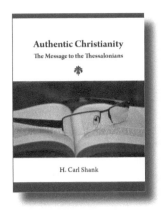

Authentic Christianity: The Message to the Thessalonians,
2019.

We are in desperate danger of making Christianity fit our
culture rather than transforming that culture by its radical,
life changing message and demands. As Patrick Morley
points out, "There is a God we want and there is a God who
is. They are not the same God. Cultural Christianity means
to seek the God we want instead of the God who is. By
default, people become cultural Christians when they do
not proactively choose to become biblical Christians."

Os Guinness writes that we live in an age of "post-
truth," making Christianity fit our experiences and cultures.
Paul's message to the Thessalonian Church is all about
authenticity — authentic conversion, authentic Christian
service, authentic encouragement, authentic lifestyles and
authentic expectation of the second coming of Jesus Christ.

Available from lulu.com and amazon.com and other
booksellers.

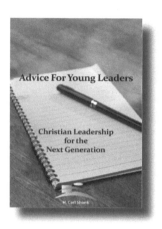

Advice for Young Leaders: Christian Leadership for the Next Generation, 2018.

Francis Schaeffer once said and wrote that we live and minister before a "watching world." The non-Christian world often wants us to stumble and falter and fail. They want committed believers in Jesus Christ to betray their Lord and Savior. They watch for it, wait for it and then report it when it happens as evidence of moral and institutional failure and sickness. The real question for those daring to enter into full-time professional ministerial service for the Lord Jesus Christ is how do I not fall and finally fail my Lord and Savior? How do I make sure that my ministry years will be biblically fruitful and that I will remain faithful to Christ? How can I leave a legacy of godliness and faithfulness that others can follow safely and surely? This book explores some of the answers to those questions.

Available from lulu.com and amazon.com and other booksellers.

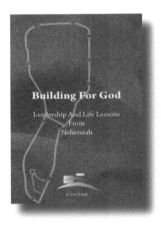

Building For God: Leadership and Life Lessons from Nehemiah, A Bible Study, 2018.

Nehemiah was an unknown servant to a great ancient Near Eastern king, a cupbearer by trade. He was not a famous Jewish prophet, scribe or known leader. Yet, through this man, the torn down and burnt walls of Jerusalem were rebuilt in an amazing fifty-two days. He faced opposition and ridicule by the appointed leaders on the ground in and around Jerusalem. He had to deal with recalcitrant people, scared people and lazy, unproductive people. He had to conquer unfair business practices and engineer conflict resolution, all while facing enemies from a secular empire.

Available from lulu.com and amazon.com and other booksellers.

Church Warnings! The Seven Churches of Revelation for Today, A Bible Study, 2017.

A Bible study with Teacher Notes and discussion guide on the seven churches cited in Revelation 2–3. Christ's messages to the seven churches of Revelation are as relevant today as they were then. Ephesus-like churches who have "forsaken their first love," and churches like Pergamum and Thyatira which tolerate false teachers and teaching, as well as churches like Sardis and Laodicea who are lackadaisical about the faith are in danger. Churches like Smyrna and Philadelphia who have endured much persecution are told to hold on and overcome. To all seven, Jesus says, "He who has an ear, let him hear what the Spirit says to the churches."

Available from lulu.com and amazon.com and other booksellers.

Jonah: A Reluctant Messenger, A Needy People, and God's Amazing Grace, A Bible Study, 2017.

A Bible study and discussion guide on the Old Testament story of Jonah. Grace transforms everything it touches. It does not discriminate, based on race, tradition, church experience, selectability, preference, timing or worth. There is no sin so great that grace cannot conquer and transform. There is no life so lost that grace cannot find and reclaim it. There is no one so wicked or unworthy that grace cannot totally change and renovate. This study of Jonah shows God's amazing, mighty and magnificent grace.

Available from lulu.com and amazon.com and other booksellers.

Romans: The Glory of God As Seen in the Righteousness of God, A Thematic Bible Study, 2017.

A Bible study book on Romans with Leader's Notes. The study is arranged according to the themes of Paul's Letter to the Romans. "Righteousness From A Sovereign God," "Universal Guilt," "Gospel Benefits," "Sanctification: God's Picture of Righteousness In Our Lives," "Sovereignty: God's Sovereignty Leads to Grateful Praise and Gospel Love," "Understanding God's Sovereign Purposes," "God Is Not Through With Israel," "Living Sacrifices," "The Politically Correct Christian," and "Liberty Not License."

Available from lulu.com and amazon.com and other booksellers.

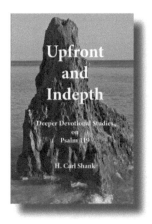

Upfront and Indepth: Deeper Devotional Studies on Psalm 119, 2010.

This little exposition of Psalm 119 unlocks some of the deeper truths of the longest Psalm recorded in the Bible. Not for the tame, or for a quick read, this devotional study will challenge you to personally go places you have never visited within your own walk with God.

Available from lulu.com and amazon.com and other booksellers.

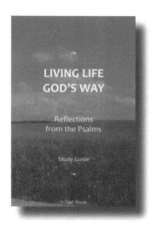

Living Life God's Way: Reflections from the Psalms, 2016.

This is a study guide for selected Psalms from the Bible. It's fill-in-the blanks format is perfect for a small group study, or even a personal study of the Psalms. It references 67 of the most read Psalms and includes a special study of Psalm 1. A selection of "Psalms for Christmas" is included in the study.

Available from lulu.com and amazon.com and other booksellers. A *Leader's Guide* is also available.

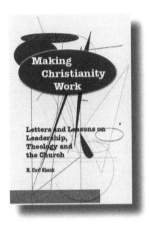

Making Christianity Work: Letters and Lessons on Leadership, Theology and the Church, 2012.

Insights shared by the author from letters, emails and various mentoring situations involving a number of lay and professional ministry leaders over an almost forty year span. Sections include "Feelings About God and Life," "Knowing God Better," "Faith and Culture," "On Church Health and Growth," "On Church Difficulties," "On Preaching and Teaching," and "On Theology."

Available from lulu.com and amazon.com and other booksellers: